THE AWARENESS TRAP

EDWIN SCHUR

THE
AWARENESS
TRAP

Self-Absorption
Instead of Social Change

Quadrangle / The New York Times Book Co.

Book design: Tere LoPrete

Library of Congress Cataloging in Publication Data

Schur, Edwin M
    The awareness trap: self-absorption instead
of social change.

    Includes bibliographical references and index.
    1. Psychotherapy—Social aspects. 2. Self-
perception. 3. Social change. I. Title.
RC480.5.S356   616.8'914   75-36272
ISBN 0-8129-0627-6

For Joan,
the best of friends

Contents

PART TWO. APPLICATIONS AND ABUSES

THE AWARENESS TRAP

Introduction:
The Awareness Craze

Self-awareness is the new panacea. Across the country, Americans are frantically trying to "get in touch" with themselves, to learn how to "relate" better, and to stave off outer turmoil by achieving inner peace. The sites of this activity are many: Colorado mountain tops, Kansas penitentiaries, religious retreats in Massachusetts, "growth" centers in New York and California; and ordinary homes and working places throughout the nation. Methods and resources for this self-exploration are similarly various: Feelings-oriented "rap sessions" modeled on the encounter groups of the 1950s and 1960s. Ideas and practices drawn from ancient religious traditions of the East—such as meditation and yoga-type body disciplines. Relaxation and body-monitoring schemes (including biofeedback—the machine monitoring of brainwaves, in hopes of gaining conscious control of emotions). To a limited extent, the expansion of perception through consciousness-altering drugs. A host of "new therapies," among them Primal Scream, Gestalt (focusing on the "whole person"), Transactional Analysis (including exploration of "games people play"). And combining an assortment of self-awareness ideas in popular form, a steady stream of simplistic psychological self-help books.

Each theory or practice has its unique features. Devotees of any one scheme may well object to my lumping their approach together with others. But there are important interconnections and common elements. These seemingly diverse activities are manifestations of a broader social movement. This is not any sort of intentional conspiracy. Nor is it even a coherent and unified effort to achieve specifiable goals. Rather, it amounts to a diffuse but clearly emerging cultural tendency. A general trend that is more and more a major influence on our ways of thinking and of acting. My focus in this book is on the common themes and connecting links found within this trend. And not so much on the specific practices themselves, as on the underlying assumptions and ideas that inform them. A seductively appealing, but distorted and socially harmful, ideology of awareness is rapidly gaining acceptance. If we allow this to go on, unquestioned and unchecked, we will do so at our considerable peril.

Once dominant, this ideology could push our society in highly undesirable directions. If promoters of self-awareness claimed only that they could make individuals feel healthier and more "alive," there might be little problem. But many of them go well beyond this limited goal. They see "personal growth" as the key to social progress. Becoming "aware" as the path to good interpersonal relations, and the solution to numerous social problems—national, and even international, in scope. Health, education, and welfare; family, work, and government—all will miraculously grow and change for the better as we get more in tune with ourselves and the people around us.

These claims rest on serious misconceptions as to how

people live and social change occurs. They imply that somehow human beings can act and interact within a social and
moral vacuum. That social structures and forms are meaningless and unnecessary. That unhappiness is due to our not
realizing our true selves. That "openness" and honesty will
cause conflict and discontent to disappear. That learning
certain content-free interpersonal skills will help ensure that
we lead satisfying lives. That the very process of experiencing
is more important than what it is that we experience. Part
One of this essay examines these ideas, and shows how
vacuous and misleading they tend to be. In Part Two, I consider a variety of substantive areas in which such formulations
have been applied. There we will see the patent inadequacy
(and at times, retrogressive implications) of approaching the
real problems facing our society in self-awareness terms.

If I have just stated the new credo in what may seem an
exaggerated form, this is nothing next to the glib claims and
snap formula-making of recent awareness popularizers.
Throughout my discussion, I draw extensively on statements
made by these mass-marketed writers. Some of their books
are quite simpleminded, and it is easy to make fun of them.
In fact, several parodies already have appeared. But it would
be a serious mistake to ignore the potential impact of these
works. They are not best sellers for nothing. They incorporate
the most successful themes of the awareness outlook. The
millions of Americans who read them are not doing so for
entertainment alone.

Especially in these popularizations, we see that the current
interest in awareness strongly reflects our culture's long-standing emphasis on individualism and self-help. It has much in
common with a variety of earlier self-reliance philosophies
and "popular religions"—ranging from the writings of Ralph
Waldo Emerson to those of Norman Vincent Peale. (See
Chapter III.) Unlike some of their forerunners, the current
tracts play down the conventional work ethic and competition
for monetary success. Instead they emphasize what might be

called psychological success. But the insistence that we can all help ourselves, that once we've been aimed in the right direction we can carry through, is standard fare in this genre. Even in the more theoretical works on the new awareness, a similarly casual optimism prevails—tied to the notion that we must all accept "responsibility for ourselves." We cannot expect other people to solve our problems for us. By the same token, we cannot solve theirs.

Along with the stress on continuously exploring one's feelings, this represents a clear invitation to self-absorption. The latent political implication seems equally apparent: complacency for those who have succeeded; resignation or self-blame for those who have not. As we shall see, from the standpoint of seriously disadvantaged segments of our population—the poor, racial and ethnic minorities, women, people labeled "deviant"—the awareness movement offers a particularly inadequate type of "liberation." Some of its methods may have specific uses, for example in breaking down stereotypes, or in strengthening self-respect and personal assertiveness. But it does not begin to deal with institutionalized oppression, which is very real to these people.

It may be true, as some have argued, that what really "grabs" the average person is a reassessment of his or her own condition. Women's consciousness-raising (see Chapter V) offers a way of combining such personal evaluation with awareness of the broader social context. Partly it works by leading women to redirect their own lives. But its real political impact lies in alerting them to the institutional nature of oppression, and getting them to do something about it. Self-awareness specialists usually show no signs of recognizing that a reconstruction of social institutions is necessary if we are to change the way we live.

Oppression is not—as they seem to believe—simply a matter of certain individuals behaving in unloving or unliberated ways. It is systematic, socially structured, and culturally reinforced. To understand and change it, we usually will need to focus on a great many sociocultural factors—ranging from economic structure to the mass media, from status hierarchies to the legal system, from employment opportunities to child-rearing attitudes. When problems transcend the personal or interpersonal levels, so too must the solutions. This is perfectly clear to the black man unable to find a job, or the woman denied a legal abortion. In such situations, no amount of self-awareness will suffice.

The awareness movement's appeal for Americans today is not hard to fathom. When confronted by external confusion, threat, or crisis, people are tempted to withdraw into themselves. This tendency may be heightened by living under the sway of large-scale bureaucracy and technology. If taking time out—to imagine and feel, to explore ourselves and our natural surroundings—will enable us to escape the proverbial rat race, we may grab at the chance eagerly. Dissatisfaction with our interpersonal relationships also contributes to the appeal. Puritanism and a commitment to rationality may have unnecessarily inhibited our spontaneity and direct enjoyment of sensual pleasure. Then too, pressure to conform socially has many people wondering whether they have been playing roles rather than really living their own lives.

There is also a deeper appeal. To have caught on the way they have, awareness outlooks must have struck more basic notes in the American character. Part of this concordance lies in the aforementioned themes of individualism and personal responsibility. In addition the new self-exploration meshes well with our cultural proclivity for seeking the easy path. Unlike Freudian psychoanalysis, it does not require a time-consuming effort to reconstruct personal history and understand an intricate web of meaning. Unlike the esoteric disciplines of the Orient, American adaptations need not involve a thoroughgoing commitment to any culturally grounded spiritual tradition. Finally the delusive belief that individual growth will automatically produce major social change jibes nicely with our typically apolitical and ahistorical ways of viewing the world.

The excitement about self-awareness has also provided yet

another outlet for the ceaseless entrepreneurialism of Americans. Alvin Toffler was right on the mark when he forecast (in his book *Future Shock*) the rise of "experiential" industries—"whose sole output consists not of manufactured goods, nor even of ordinary services, but of pre-programmed 'experiences.' "[1] As well as being highly profitable, the new movement has a self-propagating or self-propelling quality. Most awareness schemes disdain formal credentials, and at the same time generate disciples. Under these conditions, "graduates" easily see themselves as qualified to set up programs of their own. These programs in turn expand, and produce still more program-propagating disciples.

As a result, we see the rapid proliferation of comprehensive "growth centers" that offer the awareness-consumer everything and anything. One recent announcement (for Anthos, in New York) touted, "Workshops on sexuality, relating, primal feelings, primal-gestalt, freeing the creative process, couples group, separation and divorce, gestalt, self-definition, and others." Another (for Arica) offered summer residential "training centers" in eleven locations (in the U.S., the Caribbean, South America, and Europe): "The curriculum is a comprehensive set of precisely balanced techniques, including exercise, dance and movement for the physical body, meditation, mantram, individual analysis assignments, and other work to balance and harmonize mind, body, and emotions."[2]

Along with the current resurgence of mass-distributed personal guidance books, the popularity of such (fee-charging) programs signifies the existence of a large awareness market. Colleges too have heard this message, particularly those emphasizing adult education. Such programs, geared to non-matriculated students, now typically offer a wide array of self-realization courses. At one New York institution recently, the following were but a few of them: "Workshop in Group Therapy," "Intimacy and Close Relationships in Action," "On Being a Separate Person," "Toward Self-Understanding II," and "Understanding the Struggle to be 'ME.' "[3]

Only a leisure class can afford to devote so much time, energy, and money to self-exploration. As we shall see, it is to such a class and its typical problems that the movement's basic appeal is directed. And far from inciting a break with our dominant patterns of competitive consumption (as some awareness-oriented idealists had hoped would happen), the "new consciousness" has itself become a commodity. It is being heavily promoted, packaged, and marketed, much like any other commercial item. While the movement provides middle-class consumers with an attractive new product, attention is diverted from the more serious social problems that plague our society—poverty, racism, environmental decay, crime, widespread corporate and governmental fraud.

Many of the qualities prized by awareness advocates are admirable. Presumably we would all like to be honest, spontaneous, and authentic, and to achieve our own aims without disadvantaging other people. Similarly, it's hard to disagree with most of their criticisms of the general quality of our present-day lives. We need to increase genuine feelings of community, temper our national obsession with power and material success, reevaluate cultural priorities and revamp social institutions. However, the current awareness movement often seems to be pushing us away from these qualities and goals at least as much as toward them. Its limited interiorizing concepts, virulent commercialization, and ridiculously excessive claims encourage people to withdraw from the political and social actions that are needed—regardless of what early awareness enthusiasts may have had in mind. By inviting us to become preoccupied with our "selves" and our sensations, it is diluting our already-weak feelings of social responsibility. And, ironically, in its approach to "relationships" (Chapter IV) it may be encouraging manipulative behavior of precisely the sort it claims to abhor.

It urges us to take life seriously, in the sense of not letting it pass us by. But there is every indication that these new helpers do not really comprehend the seriousness of life. Nobody reasonable objects to personal pleasure, to the enhancement of every individual's experiencing of life. However life is more than just a collection of feeling individuals. It is inherently social and political. It crucially involves reaching out, as well as looking in. Somehow these facts are eluding the self-awareness movement. Even for those who can afford to try out all its fancy techniques and peppy formulas, the long-term payoff is bound to be inadequate. Eventually awareness enthusiasts will be forced to face the fact that they have (quite literally) been sold a false bill of goods.

Part One / THINKING IN AWARENESS TERMS

1 / Feeling Your Feelings

Back to Nature

A hallmark of the awareness outlook is that we should just be natural. We should return to basics. The difficulty, of course, lies in knowing what is natural and basic, and how to get there. Self-awareness specialists often seem confident that they have the answers. They claim our daily experience represents but a highly impoverished version of what life can be like. Life, in short, can be beautiful. The basic reason it isn't is that we have settled for such an inadequate substitute. Inadequate because it simply isn't real.

Behind these ideas lurks a vague romantic conception of real living, and excessive optimism about what can be accomplished through reasserting "the organic unity of the individual and nature," as it's often put. According to Claudio Naranjo, it is time for us to be "abandoning forms and search-

ing for the essence that animates them, an essence which
often lies hidden in the forms themselves."[1] One might well
agree that there are a great many forms we should indeed
abandon. The problem remains, however, whether one can do
away with forms entirely. What then would be left? Presumably, that "essence." Yet this mysterious entity continues
to elude philosophers and gurus, along with more empirically
minded investigators. Naranjo himself elsewhere refers cryp-
tically to "a need which seeks a nourishment words can only
hint at."[2]

Much of the motivation behind the call for getting back to
basics is reasonably sound. (Though often it's stated in exaggerated form.) We are said to have become artificially split
off from intimate connection with ourselves and our natural
environment—literally, out of touch and out of tune with our
humanity, and with the natural world. We are surrounded by
material possessions, obsessed with meeting externally imposed standards, overstimulated by cultural distractions, overwhelmed by meaningless tasks performed in alienating settings. These circumstances, we are told, have deprived us of
our sense of wonder. We have lost all feeling for the ele-
mental and eternal verities of nature.

According to proponents of the new awareness, we experience life almost exclusively in indirect and secondary ways.
Other people tell us what to do. We also let them (the so-
called experts) tell us what we ourselves and the world around
us are like. Our direct perceptions have been distorted by an
overlay of preconceived interpretations. As a result, our sense
of reality only taps a narrow vein of the wealth of direct
experience we could potentially mine. We are so preoccupied
with these secondary processes—interpreting, rationalizing,
classifying, and organizing—that we fail to appreciate the
essential unity of life.

To overcome these tendencies we need, it is said, a new
kind of revolution. According to Theodore Roszak, we must
"liberate the visionary powers from the lesser reality in which

they have been confined by urban–industrial necessity."[3] This
means a return to directness. To feelings, instead of words
describing feelings. To unity and wholeness, instead of distinction-drawing and categorizing. To fluidity and process,
instead of a false and static sense of finality. To wonder, instead of ungrounded certainty. To life affirmation, instead of
deadening routinization.

Some awareness-oriented writers see a new connection with
the natural environment as the key to such change. Roszak, in
his book *Where the Wasteland Ends,* writes eloquently of
the need to surmount "the artificial environment." He and
others have argued that the growing environmental concern
and the self-awareness quest should feed into each other. So
far, however, the link seems tenuous at best.

A Canadian writer, Robert Hunter, has suggested that environmental decay is the one issue on which all the dissident
elements in our type of complex society can agree. Since the
environment affects everyone, potential conflicts will be
muted and a unified social movement will become possible.[4]
Both Roszak and Hunter are strong enthusiasts for the growing focus on self-awareness. To them, the environmental crisis
is the cutting edge of the new-style revolution that will produce a more general change in consciousness. Deterioration
of the natural environment will force us to recognize the
bankruptcy of our prevailing technology, and to explore alternative ways of knowing and acting. And as we do this, we
will develop still greater regard for our natural surroundings—
which, in turn, we will then make greater efforts to nurture
and sustain.

These are attractive predictions. However, there are few
signs that all this is really about to happen. To be sure, particularly among segments of American youth, a new appreciation of nature seems evident. Witness the renewed interest
in farming and "homesteading," and also the enormous popularity of health foods. The recent communes too, are predominantly rural, and can be seen as part of a "back to the

land" movement. But are these trends significantly encouraged by the movement for self-awareness? It does not
seem so, given the dominant direction that movement has
been taking.

Contemplativeness and enhanced appreciation of nature
may tend to go together. Quite probably it is true that all too
often our attitude toward the environment has been one of
apparent hostility. As Alan Watts puts it, "The hostile attitude of conquering nature ignores the basic interdependence
of all things and events—that the world beyond the skin is
actually an extension of our own bodies—and will end in
destroying the very environment from which we emerge and
upon which our whole life depends."[5] Overcoming or at least
tempering this hostility is a commendable goal. But the main
thrust of recent self-fulfillment activities is not toward achieving it.

The environmental crisis nicely illustrates the awareness
movement's potential and its limitations. In this area, as in so
many others, we see that a new individual consciousness—if
widespread enough—could activate pressures for change. By
itself, however, it could scarcely begin to effectuate the many
kinds of change that are needed. Searching for what is real
in themselves and the world around them may lead some
people to feel a new reverence for nature. A few may then
take personal action in its behalf. But significant environmental change requires a large-scale and well-focused collective effort. It requires revising or reversing current public
policies and altering dominant social institutions. Fragmented
instances of self-awareness will not be adequate to this task.

Utopians or visionaries (depending on your viewpoint)
stress the implicit link between self-realization and remaking
the environment. Most of the popularized awareness tracts,
however, are silent on this issue. Similarly, the hordes of middle-class yoga enthusiasts, rap-session devotees, and other
growth-program consumers, are not about to throw themselves into radical action on the environmental front. There
may well be a logical sequence from a focus on self-awareness

to concern with personal well-being, to awareness of health problems and their sources in our treatment of the environment. Yet a logical sequence is not necessarily an actual one. Whether a new consciousness will actually promote the kind of self-activation needed to alter highly entrenched social priorities remains to be seen.

Consider, for example, the growing interest in so-called health foods. New outlooks on the relation between people and nature have helped bring this trend about. And eating better food undoubtedly makes those who do so, in turn, feel better about themselves and what nature has to offer. Yet these outlooks and actions alone can only take us so far. Food growers and processors, distributors and promoters are all important focal points for action directed at really significant change. Governmental assistance and legislative directives and controls are needed, along with massive changes in social values and preferences. It could be argued that once we all demand healthful foods they will be made available. In a sense this is correct. But generating a collective consciousness of this sort presupposes a far-reaching program of education, with facts, figures, and arguments.

By the same token, vested interests in existing priorities and in particular food products will not simply disappear because of some new feeling about self and nature. Obstacles to turning our food consumption in a more healthful direction are especially apparent when one considers the role of advertising and the place of children in this domain. Children usually eat what their parents give them to eat, but frequently (in our society) they tell their parents what it should be. And what it should be they've learned, to a great extent, from television. Even if adults were immune to the constant bombardment of advertising for brand-name food products (including "junk food"), children could hardly avoid being affected by it. The parent-pestering that results cannot easily be resisted.

So the media and advertising industries are at once implicated in the situation we wish to change. Under a system such as ours that so venerates profit-making, the aim, furthermore, is to produce and distribute at low cost regardless of health value. This tendency too must be faced up to by advocates of change. And this is all without even taking into account the ramifications of persisting poverty. For the really poor among us, the urgent goal is not health food, but just plain food. In such circumstances, it is hard to concentrate on abstract long-term benefit.

Ultimately, then, the question of health foods—like other specific policy issues to be considered throughout this book—involves myriad aspects of our socioeconomic order. Self-awareness may propel individuals into actions aimed at producing meaningful change. It can initiate and activate, but by itself—at least in the absence of a widely shared sense of collective interests and goals—it cannot accomplish much more. Potentially it is a significant generator of change. Whether it will fulfill this potential, however, depends on the extent to which individuals caught up in the awareness-enhancing process can move beyond its built-in limitations. Perhaps we should distinguish between experiencers and activists. Certainly it is possible to be both, but emphasis on one mode may be largely at the expense of the other.

At present, the self-awareness movement is encouraging us to become a nation of "direct experiencers." This need not preclude active pursuit of social and political goals, but the danger is that the very process of experiencing will itself envelop us. An exclusive focus on the personal and interpersonal levels of human experience encourages that result. When the path back to basics takes an inward direction, it tends to inhibit sociopolitical action. The experiencing of experience (recapturing a sense of basic "process") that is lauded as a new consciousness becomes, then, a distinct drawback.

Becoming Open

This basic process is often described as "freeing up" or "becoming open." Another extremely common awareness notion is "liberation." To what should we be open? And from what (and for what) should we be liberated? It is common to speak of freedom and liberation in social, political, or intellectual terms. But in this context the emphasis is on something else entirely. Each person should try to achieve a (rather vaguely defined) psycho-emotional freedom and liberation. The focus is on releasing the "inner person." Similarly, openness does not mean being receptive to new ideas, outlooks, or social situations. Rather we are to be open to ourselves, to the feel of our immediate surroundings, and to the responses and vibrations of other people with whom we are in direct contact.

Hence what might be truly liberating—a broadening of perspectives as well as a heightening of sensation—often turns, in this interiorized version, into a narrowing of the individual's outlook. On the other hand, in some circles a nebulous concept of openness becomes a kind of fetish. We should be open to everything and anything, to everyone and anyone. In other words, totally undiscriminating. In a sense, this is what awareness-makers really want. It follows from their aim of breaking down our perpetual distinction-making and analyzing, from condemning our tendency to rationally assess all our experience (that is, "discriminate" by imposing standards, asserting values, and making choices). Yet even intellectual openness can, if carried too far, be a bad thing. Being totally open to every idea, one becomes a kind of intellectual sieve. In an ill-defined area of emotional response and self-assessment, the same approach can be truly chaotic.

Every emotion has value, according to the new ideology. We must recognize all feelings, express them, open them up to the people around us. We must, in short, "let it all hang out." If we accept this view, there seems little room for us to discriminate among our emotions or control our feelings. Awareness enthusiasts may be right that we have overcontrolled in the past. Yet it is not at all clear that undifferentiated and undiscriminating feeling is always a good thing. The cult of openness threatens those domains of psychological and emotional reserve that people rightly cherish. In his excellent study of the encounter and sensitivity movement sociologist Kurt Back emphasized the threat such programs pose to the need for and right to privacy. As he noted, "The norms of encounter groups frequently treat this right as obnoxious, and the social pressure within these groups is to persuade the person to surrender it."[6]

Back and others have expressed concern about the psychological damage that may result from such enforced openness. The danger to unstable individuals—particularly when they are at the hands of ill-trained, insensitive, or unscrupulous group leaders or fellow participants—is obvious. What obsessive openness (in the group context or any other) does for or to persons who are in pretty good psychological shape beforehand we simply do not know. Today the call for openness extends well beyond group therapy and encounter sessions. As psychologist Thomas Cottle recently pointed out, our entire society seems to be leaning toward more and more divulging and exposing, less and less confidentiality and withholding.[7] In later sections of this book, I shall consider some specific manifestations of this tendency—including the much-publicized idea of "open marriage," and the influential movement for increased openness in our schools. To the extent these developments reflect a trend toward greater honesty and equality, they are without question commendable. But when openness and liberation (or the mechanisms for achieving them) become ends in themselves, obscuring all other worthwhile goals, our society is likely to be in great trouble.

The various approaches to achieving liberation through increased self-awareness all share in the irony of purporting to teach us how to be natural. We are offered techniques for feeling our feelings, skills for developing our spontaneity, systematic methods for achieving simplicity. There are, at a minimum, three somewhat different approaches to awareness-enhancing. One is represented by the "expressivists" (including the new sensualists). A second is that of the "detachers" (they seek to achieve detachment from the world). A third is

developed by the "communicators" (who stress the importance of content-free communications skills). Although there
are complicated bodies of theory lying behind these approaches, and claims of definitiveness made by some proponents of each, they are not really mutually exclusive schools.
They differ somewhat in emphasis, but not greatly in purpose
or overall outlook. As I have mentioned, my own concern
here is with common ideas and interconnections. Some advocates of the new awareness themselves recognize that they are
all (as Claudio Naranjo stresses) engaged in, "The One
Quest." Among the major unifying themes is this business of
becoming open. In one way or another, all aim at liberating
the person.

What are the different emphases given to this common
idea? Encounter groups—by now much chronicled, at times
criticized, and according to some observers already on the
wane—are of course the prototype of the expressivist approach.
Writer Jane Howard, reporting (in *Please Touch*) on her
national participant-observation tour of encounter programs
and centers, commented favorably on their getting people to
risk "more emphasis on warmth, even at the expense of light.
Maybe we have plenty of light already."[8] Critics (such as Kurt
Back) have stressed the anti-intellectualism of these programs
(which Ms. Howard obviously recognized), the artificial
nature of the group situation, excessive claims by encounterists, and the considerable danger of misuse or abuse of their
techniques. Our main focus here, however, is on the outlooks encounter spokesmen and their proteges have been disseminating. These outlooks keep cropping up all over the
place—often quite far from actual encounter-group settings.

In his book *Joy*, an already classic statement of the encounter approach, William Schutz emphasizes that there is
no established routine to be adopted in every encounter group.
"Instead, it uses the feelings and interaction of group members as the focus of attention. The process of achieving personal growth begins with the exploration of feelings within

the group and proceeds to wherever the group members take it."[9] As he goes on to state, members are above all urged to be open and honest. Usually a feeling of group solidarity develops that helps facilitate mutual exploration. Schutz describes many specific techniques that may be used in this opening-up process, techniques that will (he claims) enhance "personal functioning." There is a great variety of possible touching and feeling exercises. Some focus on one's own feelings and body, some involve two or more group members exploring together. Some methods aim at developing trust (as when one person falls and allows himself or herself to be caught by a fellow encounterist). Others allow one to express personal hostility or affectionate feelings (actively kicking; actively hugging). Many are strongly body-oriented. Still others are specifically geared to developing competence in interpersonal relations (see Chapters IV and VI). Some seek to enhance self-understanding through exploration of fantasies and day-dreams.

By such means, the encounterists hope to release the individual's full potential. To free the body and the emotions now shackled by socially imposed inhibitions. To allow the person to feel vitality and joy through unrestricted experience and effortless functioning. To cut through the verbalizations and poses, and get to the person's "gut feelings." This last theme is an extremely important one that permeates the entire awareness movement. According to the authors of a major text on gestalt therapy, our ordinary life tends to be dominated by "word disease." We live a substitute life of verbalizing and supposedly objective analysis, rather than experiencing life itself fully and directly. "When one fears contact with actuality—with flesh-and-blood people and with one's own sensations and feelings—words are interposed as a screen both between the verbalizer and the environment and between the verbalizer and *his own organism*. The person attempts to live on words—and then wonders vaguely why something is amiss!"[10]

This quite explicit anti-intellectualism comes across repeat-

edly in the current psychological self-help literature. It is an all
too easy jump from theorizing about artificial limitations on
human potential to providing glib assurances that we can all
fulfill ourselves simply by feeling our feelings. Thus one best
seller asserts: "Awareness is an endlessly available opportunity
offering the possibilities of new discoveries of who one is and
who one isn't. This limitless potential to experience the joy
and excitement of learning about oneself and one's world can
make life a meaningful adventure for anyone."[11] These books
tend to stress heavily the nonverbal, nonanalytic expressive
paths to awareness. Often they present a variety of physical
and interpersonal "exercises" or other encounter-generated
techniques and concepts.

From a sociopolitical standpoint, the concept of human
potential so much bandied about in discussions of self-awareness is in fact a very strange and narrow one. This is a point
I discuss in more detail later in this book. But even putting
aside for the moment the question of what's missing in the
concept, we may wonder just who can take advantage of whatever real value it does have. My discussion below also makes
clear the patent class bias of the awareness movement and the
new self-help writings. It is all very well for Jerry Greenwald
to refer to awareness as an "endlessly available opportunity,"
and to depict life as "a meaningful adventure for anyone."
Without doubt he sincerely believes this.

Yet it is simply not true that this kind of personal liberation
will be of equal value to all. Some people are conspicuously
freer than others to appreciate the benefits of becoming open.
And nowadays the price of awareness may come high. As one
commentator on the new "humanistic" psychology remarks,
"the new humanists do not deal with the poor. The cost of
one marathon session would wreck the family budget of a
workingman and the cost of two would bankrupt him."[12]
Since group and encounter techniques are often proclaimed
for their cheapness and wide applicability, this is a most
paradoxical state of affairs.

"Detachers" advocate a slightly different path to becoming

open. If encounter sessions as such may be experiencing a
slight decline, the detachment approach seems to be going
strong. Witness current interest in yoga, transcendental meditation, and other Eastern derivatives. In this version of the
awareness quest, the emphasis is on filtering out all cultural
and perceptual distractions. On transcending worldly cares to
achieve serenity. Liberation through simplicity. Attainment of
some transcendent state beyond the narrow confines of conscious ego and socially conditioned perception.

Research psychologist Robert Ornstein suggests that the
process of meditation is "similar to that of taking a vacation—
leaving the situation, 'turning off' our routine way of dealing
with the external world for a period, later returning to find it
'fresh,' 'new,' 'different,' our awareness 'deautomatized.' "[13]
Our ordinary ways of thinking and talking about the world,
say the detachers (in much the same vein as the gestalt therapists) are quite inadequate. We define and categorize, instead of directly apprehending the overwhelming unity of
which we are a part. This unity has to be experienced to be
believed. Indeed, Alan Watts maintains, when one does directly experience it, "Everything fits into place in an indescribable harmony—indescribable because paradoxical in the
terms which our language provides."[14]

The claims now being made for meditation—and for other
relaxation-oriented techniques (see below)—are not modest
ones. Detachment and serenity are being offered as solutions
to everything from ulcers to international conflict. Ameri-
canized adaptations of long-standing Eastern concepts express
our culture's characteristic optimism and stress on practical
results. A good example is provided by the Maharishi Mahesh
Yogi, much revered as a Holy Man. Although the Maharishi
emphasizes the "bliss consciousness of absolute Being" that
can be achieved through transcendental meditation, at the
same time he is at pains to insist his formulations are easily
accessible, practical, and effective. He writes that "while this
Science of Being is perfect in its theory, it is also a practical

science in which results are found only when the experiment is made. It is open to every individual to experience this state of Being and create in his life a state of eternal freedom while bringing greater success in all fields of activity."[15] In a nutshell: pragmatic bliss.

Expressivists would only have us discard intellectual analysis and restrictive social forms. Detachers are closer to an ascetic tradition that encourages withdrawal from most aspects of everyday life. They seek "pure awareness" (a sense of cosmic unity), and not just natural feeling and behavior. How far this withdrawal may go is seen in another statement by Alan Watts, where he points to "that primordial repression which is responsible for the feeling that life is a problem, that it is serious, that it *must* go on. It has to be seen that the problem we are trying to solve is absurd. . . . The point is not that the problem [life] has no solution, but that it is so meaningless that it need not be felt as a problem."[16] At least potentially, then, becoming open through detachment comes close to what the psychiatrists (in diagnosing pathology) term "leaving the field."

The "communicators" comprise a somewhat less distinct component of the awareness movement. Freer and more effective communicating, after all, was one of the aims of the encounterists—whose approach in part grew out of early ideas about "group dynamics." And many self-awareness schemes emphasize the special value of group process. This may reflect a more general cultural emphasis in America today. Although we prize the individual, we may prize the individual in a group even more. Work groups, play groups, neighborhood groups, therapy groups, and even sex groups seem to be omnipresent in our type of society.

If we define communication broadly enough, most of the new self-exploration advocates are strongly interested in one or another of its forms. Even the detachers, whose approach is not very group-oriented, seem concerned to enhance some kind of communication—with one's inner self, with cosmic forces, or with the unifying processes that link humans to their environment. Perhaps the most emphasized communications–awareness link nowadays involves so-called nonverbal communication (gesture, body position, etc.). As we will see very shortly, the movement for greater self-awareness represents in high degree, and various forms, a reassertion of interest in the human body.

With respect to some specific activities, awareness theories and writings give paramount attention to communication. In industry and other organizational settings, applied social science has long employed group methods, and analysis of interaction-communication networks, with an eye to improving morale and increasing efficiency. Today, the popular literature on relationships (Chapter IV) is shot full of communications concepts and jargon. As we'll see, these books urge couples to try hard to communicate more and better, both verbally and nonverbally. If they are more open in conveying their feelings and needs, and if they learn to "read" each other more accurately, partners will be more likely to relate meaningfully. They must learn to recognize, and overcome the temptation to play, various relating games. This will help maximize authenticity and mutuality. These new relating texts treat communication as both cause and effect. When we communicate better, we become more self-aware and aware of our partners. This, in turn, will improve our general communicating and interacting abilities. Then we will be more "effective" in various relationships and situations.

This literature displays in particularly blatant form the belief that we can achieve happiness by learning and strengthening (supposedly) content-neutral skills. What you're relating or communicating about is not too important. Nor does it matter much what kind of person you or your partner proves to be. Instead the key question becomes—Are you a good communicator? As I emphasize below, in discussing the new concept of relating, this approach carries with it a dangerous invitation to adopt a manipulative interpersonal ethic. Or, really, no ethic at all. We are told to focus on our skills, on meeting our own needs. Better relating *with* the other person is turned into relating better *than* the other.

By several different paths, then, becoming "open" is held out as the key to liberating the individual. It usually means cutting through and casting off social conventions and forms. Trying to get a sense of oneself. Getting a "feel" for things, rather than just thinking them through. The basic idea is to be open to a wide variety of stimuli. What kind of stimuli? The new mentality is somewhat clearer about what it is liberating people *from*, than about what it is liberating them *for*. Even if we agree that many of our present living patterns are unsatisfactory, just what is it that greater openness will provide as an alternative?

In place of the presently undernourished modes, we are told, will be an undisturbed and direct process of engagement in the process of living. Empty forms will be replaced by totally satisfying process. Here again, in this interpretation of engagement, common usage is turned on its head. Engagement no longer means confronting the real world. The scope of living is reduced to the individual and his or her immersion in interiorized processes. Under this conception, why does one become open, liberated, or free? Apparently so one can *feel* open, liberated, or free.

Beyond that, nothing much is clear. Freedom to engage in meaningful enterprises does not seem to be part of the picture. That would involve thought, values, and goal-seeking action that reaches out in society. Despite all the talk about opening the individual up, the new self-awareness view in fact treats the individual (together perhaps with a few partners in direct interaction) as some kind of closed system. The stimuli to which one becomes open are largely one's own. At least they have meaning only in and through our direct experiencing of them. They are, in other words, sensory stimuli.

Wisdom of the Body

The awareness outlook is strongly grounded in the notion that we need to begin "listening" to our bodies. Again the specifics vary. But virtually all the recent schemes for promoting personal liberation have important biophysiological aspects. Hence the oft-repeated insistence on returning to our gut feelings. We are offered a wide range of body-related techniques that will put us in closer touch with ourselves. And in interacting with other people, too, we must let our "physical feel" for the situation guide us. Bodies are real. The supposedly sophisticated overlay of intellectual and social concepts that currently limits their use is not.

Where is the new body emphasis likely to take us? In some respects, it may prove highly beneficial. Quite probably, Americans have unnecessarily deprived themselves of freely available bodily pleasure. Our overriding commitments to getting things done, to material success and social prestige, and to rational analysis have interfered with our open enjoyment of direct sensory experience. Cultural ambivalence regarding sexuality probably has impeded the full development and appreciation of our sensual capacities. And certainly it's true that Americans do not take good physical care of themselves. We know that (when we can) we eat too much, we exercise too little, and we don't seem to know how to relax.

Self-realization techniques may help us modify some of these tendencies. However, the focus on physiology and physicality could have some unfortunate unintended consequences. By concentrating on the body, the awareness-seeker turns ever more inward. Yet life cannot realistically be reduced to physical sensation. And too great a body focus may breed a questionable kind of egocentricity. If I am really out to maximize my sensory experience, will I still be able to care about others? Indeed, will I be able to care about anything else at all? Body consciousness is one thing, body preoccupation another. The latter may signal in extreme form the drift toward anti-intellectual and antisocial withdrawal implicit in most awareness thinking.

Much of the new body ideology is captured in two special movement concepts—"somatopsychic" and "self-regulation." The former turns around the better-known idea of psychosomatic medicine (concerned with the impact of emotions on the body) to highlight possible influence of the body on the emotions. This notion is then given an applicability extending well beyond the realm of medical practice. According to this idea, our bodily condition may be determining or shaping our feelings. At the same time, our feelings may be telling us what's troubling our bodies. Psychophysiological interconnection, then, runs both ways. While our bodies reflect emotional states (which we may be able to "read" in a person's posture, expression, breathing, etc.), they can affect them as well.

William Schutz presents, as a commonsense indicator of these ties, a long and intriguing list of phrases we use in everyday conversation to describe behavior and feelings in bodily terms ("can't stomach it," "twist your arm," "turn the other cheek," and the like).[17] As I've noted, body activity is an important feature of encounter-group methods. Though it may have a considerable cathartic effect (release of hostility, for example), the aim clearly is for something more: a genuine breaking through of blocked emotions, the development of new feelings about oneself and others. Belief in a close link between body work and freeing the emotions guides all such efforts.

According to Alexander Lowen, one of the most avid proponents of the biophysiological orientation, "the soul of a man is in his body."[18] Such a notion is, of course, central to much of the Eastern philosophic-religious tradition; more specifically, to schemes in which the individual tries to develop physiological self-mastery (such as Zen, yoga, and Sufi). Physiological awareness (with or without the additional aim of developing conscious bodily control to affect feelings) is a major unifying theme of the entire awareness movement. One finds it in the "new" (Eastern-derived) religions, in encounter-grouping and other "new therapies," in a variety of schemes that are directly and primarily body oriented (see the discussion of Lowen's work that follows), and in the new laboratory "psychology of consciousness."

Some enthusiasts say we resist these efforts because of a culturally conditioned distaste for the human body and its basic workings. Quite a few encounter techniques—such as touching or sensing all parts of one's own body or someone else's, and "crotch eyeballing" (close examination of each other's genitals)—aim at overcoming inhibitions of this sort. It may seem a bit strange, however, to speak of a general cultural reticence in this area at a time when our advertising, mass media, creative arts, and popular entertainments are all so blatantly infused with body consciousness. At any rate, there is another at least equally important reason to urge caution regarding "wisdom of the body" pronouncements. It is the rather mystical context in which they often appear.

Nowadays even empirically oriented scientists are throwing such caution to the winds. Robert Ornstein, a lucid explicator of recent studies on the nature of consciousness, asserts: ". . . we should at least hold open the possibility that Western science has overlooked a subtle source of internal body energies, as the stars may be missed in the brilliance of the daylight. We may in fact be at a state of knowledge about these energies similar to that of physics just before electricity was discovered, made explicit, and harnessed."[19] Although concepts like "subtle body energies" and physiological self-mastery tend to run counter to our rationalist and materialist inclinations, at the same time (perhaps especially among the young today) they do exert a considerable fascination.

It is this fascination that, at the "outer" reaches, encourages interest in ESP, astrology, psychokinesis (moving objects through psychic powers), and other-worldly spiritualism.

Hope for some all-universe-electric solution to life may help explain the rapid diffusion of the term "vibrations." The constant talk about "vibes" draws not only on the culture of drug use and electronic rock music. It also has roots in the experimental psychology of consciousness, and in the religious and "therapeutic" references to the unity of humans-as-organisms-in-their-environment. A world consisting of personal, interpersonal, and universal vibes, along with a belief in bodily mastery of life, brings us close to the ultimate internalized version of American individualism: Do-it-yourself, through feelings and body control.

Here again, we see the attempt to provide rapid-fire all-encompassing success mechanisms. According to two enthusiastic students of biofeedback, "The ultimate possibilities for man's self-control are nothing less than the evolution of an entirely new culture where people can change their mental and physical states as easily as switching channels on a television set."[20] In a similar vein, the authors of a widely noted book praising transcendental meditation refer to "a solution to the myriad problems of our society [that] lies in the widespread application of a technique to psychophysiologically strengthen the individual and unfold his untapped resources."[21] The American proclivity to oversimplify and at the the same time overextend is, it seems, virtually unlimited.

Methods which promise physical and emotional relaxation have an understandable appeal. Our way of life is, if nothing else, overhurried and overtense. Under these conditions tension-reducing schemes find a ready audience. Many of the current meditation, and body-manipulation practices are based on one or another variant of a tension or stress theory of human problems. Referring to the "pathophysiology of modern man," the proponents of "TM" quoted earlier insist that, "Because of the total interdependency of bodily, emotional, and mental process, stress affects every phase of one's life."[22] Not surprisingly, they claim that stress reduction through deep meditation provides the answer to everything from heart attacks to poor work habits, from sleep disorders to crime. As we will see, such claims are advanced without adequate evidence (at least for the alleged "social" effects). Nor are they accompanied by a convincing statement of the mechanisms of change by which such far-reaching results could occur. Rather, they must be taken on faith. And, though the stress reducers recognize that we live in the kind of society that breeds stress, it is only the symptom of stress itself they would attack (through the body)—not its root causes in the social order.

What about the other basic physiological notion of "self-regulation"? This idea is developed particularly in gestalt therapy, which asserts as a central principle "organismic self-regulation." Fritz Perls, the father of the gestalt approach, asserts that, "The organism knows all. We know very little."[23] Another statement on gestalt (holistic) theory refers to an "integrated and coherent mode of operating in the world [that] can be observed in all living things," and a "complex process of attaining, losing, and regaining biological balance." If the organism is undisturbed, this writer contends, it will function "with a prudence born of its needs and their fulfillment."[24] This is all very well. But if organisms are self-regulating, why then do we need all of these techniques to help us regulate ourselves? If the body really is so "wise," shouldn't it be able to get along fine on its own?

Apparently the answer is twofold. That would be true if social conditions were optimal, which they are not. And anyway (partly on account of such conditions) we are failing as human beings to "listen to" and heed the body's wisdom. We have, literally, been brainwashed into not listening. This is part of what awareness specialists mean when they use the word "character" in a derogatory sense. We have, they argue, been programmed ("external regulation") to avoid the messages sent us by the body—programmed to fit into socially prescribed patterns that run against our organic needs. Hence, we find Perls maintaining that "the richest person, the most productive, creative person, is a person who has *no* character. In our society, we *demand* a person to have a character, and especially a *good* character, because then you are predictable, and you can be pigeonholed, and so on."[25]

Self-regulation is, it seems, an extremely slippery concept. Presumably such a state of affairs will pertain when the organism is in its natural setting. But when will that be? Once again, the theory bogs down because it glibly assumes the possibility of these truly natural conditions; or, alternatively, that we can simply avoid or ignore their absence, that we can be natural in an unnatural setting. Theories of tension release and self-regulation fit in nicely with a simplistic kind of closed-system equilibrium model of the human being. When anything serves to disrupt the balance of the individual, natural forces will go to work to correct the imbalance. Although this kind of automatic-checking mechanism is supposed to refer to the person-environment combination, "environment" for these purposes somehow does not include the real social structures and processes that impinge on our everyday behavior. This is, in other words, a balance in the abstract, a "naturalness" achieved in a (totally hypothetical) social vacuum.

Without reshaping these broader social structures and processes, tensions are nonetheless expected to disappear. Arthur Janov, whose "primal therapy" involves reliving (with as much emotion as possible) the traumatic experiences of early childhood, insists such techniques can produce "a tensionless, defense-free life in which one is completely his own self and experiences deep feeling and internal unity. . . . People become themselves and *stay* themselves."[26] Most current awareness literature similarly puts the pressure to change on the individual. Jerry Greenwald (in his best-selling *Be the Person You Were Meant to Be*), develops his own version of the organic-physiological motif. He suggests there are basically two kinds of people in the world: *N people* (who for the most part function in a "nourishing" way), and *T people* (pre-

dominantly "toxic" in outlook and behavior). Most of his
book is given over to prescribing "antidotes" to what he sees
as mainly "self-induced toxicity," through which people can
become more "nourishing."[27]

One of the most comprehensive efforts to develop the biophysiological theme is that of Alexander Lowen. His "bioenergetics" aims at enhancing personal fulfillment through
body-awareness and a regime of purportedly emotion-freeing
and relaxation-inducing exercises. Lowen sums up his approach in a recent book appropriately titled *Pleasure*. In
Lowen's view, we have lost our natural capacity for pleasure.
We may frantically pursue what we think will bring us pleasure. But our culture is so "ego-oriented" (geared to rational
mastery of life) that we neglect the seat of all real pleasure—
the human body. Lowen discusses diverse sources of pleasure,
but he claims all of them, in the last analysis, have a biophysiological grounding. Physical and mental health, creativity, beauty and grace, lovingness and good interpersonal
relationships, sexual pleasure, the overcoming of unhealthy
power seeking, pleasure in work, and even thinking—all these
depend on releasing the now artificially restricted potential for
sensing and enjoying our bodies.[28]

Self-awareness, according to Lowen, is a function of feeling,
and "what a person really feels is his body." Awareness is "the
summation of all body sensations at any one time." Undoubtedly it is true that most of us are "poor breathers," that
our capacity for free-flowing movement often is frozen, that
numerous repressions and suppressions prevent us from releasing all our hostilities, or fully experiencing sexual ecstasy. As I
have already agreed, almost all of us could use some loosening
up. But the biophysicalists are not content to leave it at that.
The extreme reductionism into which self-awareness thinking
deteriorates is clear from some of the further applications of
this body-oriented outlook.

Even the very basic and necessarily somewhat "internal"
matter of feelings is interpreted in an excessively narrow way.

For example, breathing is said to "create" feelings. There is no inkling that emotional responses may represent feelings *about* something or someone; that feelings have objects. On the contrary, the whole business is interiorized. Feelings are something inside us, with no external referents—neutral entities, for which we have some kind of general capacity or (trained) incapacity. Objects are interchangeable or irrelevant. We either feel or we don't feel.

Applications in other realms suggest even more strongly the limitations of this approach. Take the matter of work. It may well be true that certain kinds of work create pleasure through physical activity. The carpenter, as Lowen puts it, may find his work pleasurable because of "the coordinated movements of his body." Even leaving aside the fact that there may well be many awkward carpenters, or that not all carpenters may enjoy their work, the reduction of work (or the positive side of work) to sheer physicality drains it of all meaningful substance. Many people are discontented in their work because the tasks they must perform seem meaningless. But by the same token, work becomes pleasurable when it takes on meaning, when it permits a sense of accomplishment. Exercise and coordination may help, but they are not enough. The case of housework shows how far Lowen is prepared to carry his argument. He states, "The woman who finds pleasure in cleaning actually enjoys the physical work involved. She gives herself to the task graciously, and her movements are relaxed and rhythmical." To expect this graciousness and rhythm to move feminists, or career women, or (above all) the hard-pressed yet much-ignored working-class homemaker, is to expect a great deal indeed.

Lack of interest in specific content pervades all of Lowen's extensions of the physiological theme. We enjoy conversations, he claims, because they allow us to express our feelings and to respond to those of the other person. "The voice, like the body, is a medium through which feeling flows, and when this flow occurs in an easy and rhythmic manner, it is a pleasure both to the speaker and listener." Even thinking itself derives largely from feeling. The person who is out of touch physically cannot think in a creative manner. Here we find with a vengeance the self-awareness credo of getting "out of our heads." If thinking can be located "below the neck," then anything and everything can be reduced in similar fashion.

Persuaded by such a credo, a great many Americans spend increasing amounts of time conscientiously trying to meditate, performing prescribed exercises, watching machines register their alpha waves (brainwaves reflecting an especially tranquil state) so that they can try by conscious control to maximize them. Giving each other massages; charting their daily body rhythms (noting when and how often they eat, sleep, walk, defecate, fornicate, and the like)—none of this will do most people any harm. In fact these activities may often have positive effects on individual health and vitality. The danger lies in the absurd claims for what can be accomplished through such "body work," and even more seriously, in the reinforcement such approaches provide to oversimplified views of social life in general.

Usually the call to this new physicality pays lip service to the goal of a more life-enhancing social order. However, it adopts a romantically optimistic conception of people's natural instincts, as well as an unrealistic view of life in society. The theme of removing emotional blocks to naturalness harks back to the work of post-Freudian psychoanalyst Wilhelm Reich. As one knowledgeable commentator on his work has noted, for Reich "Character was a kind of 'armoring,' a rigid outer shell which protected the individual from the hard knocks of reality, but at the same time limited his ability to experience life, both within and without him, in its full intensity."[29] Self-awareness boosters rarely indicate the kind of society in which such character armor would no longer be necessary. Nor do they show how such a society might be brought into being.

To the new awareness ideologists, our basic instincts are

good. Unlike orthodox Freudians, they do not emphasize the
need to control the human potential for social disruption. Yet
their view of what it is to be human paradoxically seems to
require stressing similarities between us and other animal
species. The strong interest in nonverbal communication
draws heavily on studies of the lower animals. Physicality-
pushers like Lowen typically refer to "animal ability to express
anger," or to the animal-like grace of an "aware" and freely
functioning person. Popular books on what might be called
bioanthropology (such as those of Robert Ardrey, Desmond
Morris, and Lionel Tiger) have contributed to the appeal of
this kind of reasoning.

Such works throw interesting light on how some animals
behave. But trying to make an across-the-board analogy to
humans is totally unwarranted. Throughout this book, I shall
be discussing numerous cultural and social aspects of human
life that a narrow self-awareness outlook neglects. These features reflect differences between humans and the lower animals more than similarities. They reflect our special capacities
for abstract and symbolic reasoning, for transmitting a wide
range of culture content (including ideas and values)—not
only from person to person, but from generation to generation. They reflect too our collective efforts to adapt to complex social situations. Though we have created these situations
ourselves, they now exert a substantial (and largely independent) constraint upon us. Finally, they reflect our natural
inclination to actively confront this world, as well as to seek
knowledge inwardly.

Later on, we will consider some special problems to which
the new biophysiological emphasis may contribute. Lowen,
for example, waxes poetic over the wonderful vibrations we
feel in the presence of a beautiful person. No doubt he would
insist that beauty is a deep-seated quality, that it reflects
awareness, vitality, and self-appreciation. Nevertheless an extreme body consciousness could well reinforce an undesirable
cult of physical beauty, a superficiality of just the sort aware-

ness advocates say they oppose. Likewise, as we'll also see, the recent interest in nonverbal communications ("kinesics") has led to manuals that show us how to use body language as a manipulative device. Serious advocates of self-awareness would disavow these developments. Yet to an extent they are responsible for them.

Awareness writings often charge that we are unhealthily dominated by science and technology. At the same time, however, many of the new schemes (especially those that stress physiology) refer continuously to the "new" science, copiously cite scientific authority, and make frequent use of technological or scientific terms and analogies. This should alert us to the fact that they are unlikely to free us from technological domination. On the contrary, what they frequently seem to be offering us is but a new form substituting for the old. By and large, awareness advocates sincerely believe they are helping us become free to help ourselves. And that a return to the body is a major step in this direction. It may be some time before we can tell whether this urging produces more good than harm. At any rate, it fits in well with several other major tenets of the new ideology—to which I now turn.

11 / *Achieving Sensory Success*

Pain and Joy

If we are to achieve self-awareness, the feelings we experience
must have a special quality. They must be new feelings, or old
feelings experienced in a totally new way. Because awareness
is deintellectualized and divorced from specific social contexts,
its hallmark is the achievement of exceptional emotional
states. These may be of different kinds, but all the new
schemes say we must in some manner or other transcend the
allegedly humdrum level of ordinary everyday feeling. For we
suffer, according to this view, from emotional routinization.

Sometimes (as in meditation), the exceptional feelings one
aims for are extremely serene. At other times (for example,
through psychedelic drugs), the sought-after state may be
ecstatic and fantastically "mind-blowing." Or we may seek
various combinations of new emotional effects. The basic

idea, in any case, is to achieve a sensory experience that differs from what we usually have been experiencing. Perhaps most characteristic of all is the extolling of intensity. Emotional routinization is seen not so much as a matter of our experiencing the wrong emotions, rather it is a disease of emotional tone or level.

Even the detachers, who seek an utter tranquility, emphasize a kind of intensity—at least as part of the tranquility-achieving process. An intensity of concentration, a disciplined screening-out of distractions. Indeed the ultimate void they seek might be loosely described as a sort of intensely experienced nothingness. But more typical of awareness-enhancing in general is an urging that we directly focus on and intensely express our most strongly held emotions. There is a great deal of talk about pain and joy. We need to feel more joy in our lives, to replace socially conditioned emotional blandness with a new vitality. And unless we are prepared to risk pain (as it's usually put), we will never experience joy.

We have seen that encounter-group techniques (and the gestalt theory that has helped to shape them) are grounded in this valuing of emotional expression. In his useful summary of the gestalt approach, Joel Latner states: "We emphasize the emotional aspect of experience as part of contacting the totality of our lives. Our satisfaction requires that we express ourselves adequately, commensurate with our feelings, and that our feelings be part of the mix out of which will emerge new solutions."[1] We must work through and surmount the emotional blocks that inhibit free expression. We must stop relying on the "avoidance techniques" of thinking and talking, if we are to achieve full and free personal functioning.

The invariable linking together of pain and joy reflects the general emphasis on emotional intensity (extremes, of whichever type, being preferred to moderation). It also has ties to the awareness concept of finding unity in "polarities." These "holistic" outlooks are grounded in a belief that most of the dichotomies we have been taught to see around us, or read into our experience, are false. Subject—object, self—other, orga-

nism–environment—such dualities will dissolve in the very
process of full experiencing. Hence the characteristic deplor-
ing of our tendency to differentiate and classify. Such efforts,
we are told, arbitrarily deflect our attention from the overwhelming natural unity. A similar unity, perhaps, binds together such ostensible opposites as pain and joy. In a sense
they are the same thing, or at least part of the same basic process—the process of free feeling and personal growth.

This notion permeates a wide range of current awareness
literature. In their recent book *Shifting Gears*, Nena and
George O'Neill say that Americans do not want to know
about pain—"we sweep it under the rug and lock it away
where it can't be seen." Such avoidance, they insist, is highly
dysfunctional. We can only cope with the many problems
confronting us if we acknowledge crisis and put it to work in
our own behalf. "Crisis involves risk; it is a time of danger.
But it is also a vehicle for growth. If we refuse to take the risk,
then we lose not only what we used to have . . . but also the
future. Crisis is a time of testing—but it is also a time of renewal."[2] We will see later that the O'Neills' conception as to
what constitutes pain and crisis is an extremely limited one.
But the general theme is standard in awareness thinking. One
works through pain to joy. One must plumb the emotional
depths, if one is to achieve the heights.

Most of the new self-assertiveness and "relating" manuals
(see Chapters III and IV) similarly emphasize emotional risk
and emotional intensity. Not all of these books include a great
deal of direct reference to pain. Invariably, however, they
urge the reader to express all feelings openly and actively. We
are told to shed our "uptight" diffidence and deference patterns. In order to assert ourselves we must feel strongly and
express strongly. A good statement of this intensity theme is
found in a recent book on "relating," *Intimate Feedback*. The
authors note they "would personally choose to live a fully
charged emotional life and could not tolerate an existence on
a permanent voltage reduction."[3]

Understandably, the path through pain to joy has a special

place in those awareness schemes that most strongly emphasize the link between physiology and the emotions. According
to Alexander Lowen and others who share his biopsycho-
logical tension-release orientation, working through muscular
tensions and rigidities may be a painful process—not physically painful, but emotionally. For these rigidities and tensions are said to reflect the blocking or suppressing of
emotions we cannot tolerate. The real pathology, according
to Lowen, is not pain itself but rather absence of feeling of
any kind. Pain is actually the clue that will help us realize
how to (or where to) remove the suppression of feeling
through release of tension. What one must revive, above all,
is the ability to feel. Which emotion is felt, is not so important. To Lowen, the person who is unable to cry will be
unable to experience pleasure. "We cannot recover the capacity for joy without reexperiencing our sorrow"[4]

One of the most dramatic examples of the focus on pain
and joy is Arthur Janov's now very popular "primal" approach. (Primal schemes, many "unauthorized," have proliferated to such an extent in the wake of Janov's best seller
that current editions of his book even include a "warning"
to the effect that only his Institute offers the real Primal
Therapy, and that it is improper for others to use the term
Primal "in association with any word or phrase connoting
therapy or counseling.") In line with other "new therapies,"
Janov derides excessive intellectualizing and deplores the fact
that people have lost touch with their own needs and feelings.
He shares the common emphasis on physiology (referring to
our deepest feelings as "essentially neurochemical energy").
And he sees the problems of society as largely curable through
changing the individual. But his obsession with pain—going
well beyond anything Lowen has to say—distinguishes him
from his fellow awareness-promoters.

Janov's major preoccupation is with what he calls primal
pain—those "deep hurts" that result from the early interaction
(or lack of it) between parents and children. "Primal Pains

are the needs and feelings which are repressed or denied by consciousness. They hurt because they have not been allowed expression or fulfillment. These Pains all add up to: I am not loved and have no hope of love when I am really myself." Neuroses, the argument goes, develop as "defense against excessive psychobiologic pain." According to Janov, these primal pains "become stored one by one, laminated into layers of tension surging for release." The tension caused by not coming to grips with such pain seems to plague us all. It produces, says Janov, "the driving businessman, the narcotics addict, the homosexual. . . ."[5]

Primal techniques for alleviating this condition apparently vary a good bit. Typically they culminate in an emotionally wringing effort at reenacting and literally reexperiencing (with a therapist's guidance and under preparatory conditions involving a degree of sensory deprivation) these early psychic trauma. Eventually the patient both reexperiences the pain and (simultaneously) achieves emotional release—emitting the primal scream (which may take such forms as "Daddy, don't hurt me anymore," or "Mama, I'm afraid"). The claims Janov makes for this are truly remarkable. "Post-primals" not only feel better emotionally and physically, they work better, become more intelligent, have better coordination, enjoy sex more, have nonpossessive friendships, and are never moody. In fact, he suggests, primal therapy produces in a way "a new kind of human being." Is it any wonder, if this is the case, that primal enthusiasts can see their techniques as a general solution for mankind's problems? For them, pain becomes a way of changing the world.

Just how far is it reasonable to carry the pain and joy argument? Needless to say, any claim that if only we could all start experiencing our pain and joy life's problems would evaporate is exceedingly far-fetched. On the other hand, as is true of so many of the awareness concepts, the focus on pain and joy does have a positive side. It could help counteract some culturally ingrained inhibitions on strongly expressing our emotions. Perhaps the most noteworthy example is the oft-cited social discouragement of men openly expressing their feelings (especially, through crying). But women too have often been conditioned not to express their emotions freely and fully. Recognizing this has been important to the women's movement generally (see Chapter V), as well as influencing the development of specific programs for training women in assertiveness.

Stressing the need to face up to pain might conceivably help temper our tendency to view life with overly casual optimism (a tendency at least of those Americans whose socioeconomic position permits this). But failure to recognize this parenthetical qualification, and the strange manner in which both pain and joy are defined, make this result unlikely. Reducing these concepts to a physical–emotional base strongly limits their meaningfulness. There seems to be no room at all in this approach for either "social pain" or "social joy." There is little recognition that for many among us the pains of living go well beyond psychophysiology—both in cause and manifestation. At the same time we are all depicted as pursuing our daily rounds constantly hampered by enormous amounts of bottled-up internally grounded pain. In the former case, the view is myopic. In the latter, a rather glib assumption is inappropriately extended.

Again with respect to joy, a concept potentially broad in scope is reduced for the most part to physical sensation. The argument, to be sure, is that this directly sensate experience will free us for greater enjoyment of all aspects of life. But this larger goal can easily become displaced. The path through ecstasy ends up being a path to ecstasy, and nothing more. Likewise, the effort to achieve a sense of "nothingness" falls considerably short of leading on to "somethingness."

Treating joy as exceptional feeling has the possible merit of implying that we should not settle for second-best, watered-down versions of life experience. Yet this view, along with the other physiological themes, promotes and reinforces the narrow interiorizing focus of the self-awareness movement. There is little room for the joys of accomplishment, of meaningful participation in collective effort, of achieving significant (and often long-term) social goals. By insisting on ecstasy, awareness-makers run the risk of holding out (even to those of us who are strong in socioeconomic and other personal resources) an unrealistic expectation that we can never settle for anything less.

Particularly for the less fortunate, ecstasy can become a sop. Self-awareness (enhanced through drugs, meditation, or whatever) becomes the new "opiate of the people." And as intellectual historian Russell Jacoby notes, in his excellent study *Social Amnesia*, the compulsive effort at happiness invariably tends to belie itself. "The smile buttons seek to chase from mind the daily carnage and drudgery; one smiles because the living are sad. The flaunted sensitivity survives only by an iron indifference to the general deprivation and brutalization. The whole program, in brief, is grin and bear it."[6]

Here and Now

"In my lectures in Gestalt therapy, I have one aim only: to impart a fraction of the meaning of the word *now*. To me, nothing exists except the now. Now = experience = awareness = reality. The past is no more and the future not yet. Only the *now* exists."[7] Thus began Fritz Perls, in talks given at a gestalt workshop held in 1966. This emphasis on living in the present has a central place in all personal-growth programs. It bears an obvious relation to de-emphasizing rational analysis, belief in self-regulation, and stress on sensing one's feelings and expressing them directly.

As Kurt Back has pointed out, for encounterists it reflects also a faith in the value of group process itself—without reference to any broader aims. In addition, there is a close tie-up between this present orientation and the biophysiological theme. If we are really going to heed the body's wisdom, we must do it now while the impulse is strong. In this vein, sociologist-critic Philip Slater recently suggested that, "Beneath all voluntary postponement of gratification—all voluntary inhibition, suppression of feeling, commitment to a task—lies a kind of arrogance. Setting oneself above one's own bodily responses is an act of snobbery, of satanic pride."[8]

Evidence of the presentness theme extends well beyond the group-oriented programs. Alan Watts, whose work is much revered by advocates of awareness through detachment, has written that we are "breeding a type of human being incapable of living in the present—that is, of really living." For if one is unable, he goes on, "to live fully in the present, the future is a hoax."[9] An important goal of most of the meditation techniques seems to be to blot out (transcend) the impact of time considerations. The achievement of transcendence implies eradicating thoughts of past and future, and experiencing the flux of all time directly in the vivid present. According to the Maharishi, the "absolute being" one achieves through transcendental meditation supplements, as it transcends, the necessarily relative experience of everyday life: "the art of living brings together the never-active absolute of transcendental nature with the ever-changing field of relative existence and links them together."[10] We can recognize too an intense focus on the present in the very process of engaging oneself in the task of meditating.

Similarly, recent laboratory experiments into the nature of consciousness have produced a new interest in "the intuitive mode." Up to now, supposedly, this has been obscured by our exclusive concern with its counterpart, "the intellectual mode." In its timelessness and its nonanalytical quality, the former represents another way of talking about "living in the present." Robert Ornstein uses the term "nonlineal time experience" to describe the present-centered time consciousness of the intuitive mode.[11]

These notions about experiencing life in the present have

filtered through into a wide variety of popular awareness-related tracts. One example is the record-breaking best seller, *Open Marriage* (other aspects of which I examine closely in Chapter IV). Authors Nena and George O'Neill emphasize that for your relationship to be open, "you must relate to one another in the here and now." They claim that traditional marriage has been a failure in part because it has always been geared to planning for the future. In particular it has been an arena for the attainment of material goals, rather than an on-going enjoyment of "personal growth." A couple's commitment, say the O'Neills, "should be to one another rather than to goals that may or may not be achievable." Time given over to thinking of the future or mulling over the past is "time lost in the vital present. And the loss of that present time cuts down on your awareness of what is happening between you and your mate." Security-seeking, either through endlessly acquiring material possessions, or assuming that having children will ensure the couple's lifetime commitment, prevents partners "from living in the now and from actively seeking freedom, growth and love in our relationships with our mates."[12]

A similar stress on nowness is rampant in such all-purpose psychological help books as *Be the Person You Were Meant to Be*. Author Jerry Greenwald explicitly disapproves of sheer impulsiveness. (These books invariably hedge their bets by both approving and disapproving of some specific forms or degrees of every possible behavior pattern.) But he goes on to note that, "Resolutions and programs cut off the healthy self-regulating processes that are the essence of spontaneous, easy-flowing behavior." Likewise, we have to distinguish between nourishing and toxic planning. Usually the former involves experiencing the actual excitement of working toward a goal; the latter involves too much focus on our expectations for the future. Toxic planning, says Greenwald, "is often an expression of fear of living."[13]

Emphasizing spontaneity is in keeping with the desire to

break through entrenched patterns of social conditioning to the authentic individual. To promote what is often referred to as "free functioning." As we shall see, it fits in well with the awareness perspective on social roles and the individual's "true self." Yet it is a considerable jump from this general outlook to prescribing rules (as many of the popular guides do) for living in the present. Apparently the ironic internal contradiction of spontaneity training, of intentional nowness, has not come across to some of these promoters. They push right ahead with their guidelines for supposedly freer living, their "antidotes" to the old and much-deplored routinization.

Even assuming one could teach people how to live in the present, would that necessarily be a good thing? The new self-awareness ideology attributes much human unhappiness to our failure to realize the importance of doing so. But what exactly is the evidence for this? For virtually every argument the awareness-makers might advance, a counterargument with at least as much support could be presented. Of course it is true that if at every juncture one is totally caught up in planning for some new future, there never really will be a present that one can enjoy. There is another side to this, however. For those who are perpetually imprisoned in the present (needing food now, decent housing now, jobs now), there is never likely to be any real future to which one can look with hope. "Here and now" ignores them completely.

Just as the expectation of future happiness can be an illusion, so too then can be a glorification of the present. And who is to say which will produce more human satisfaction—intense immersion in the unplanned-for experience of the moment, or the fulfillment of long-maintained and fondly held hopes? Shouldn't there be plenty of room in a person's life for both? There is no basis for claiming that there can only be one kind of orientation to the future—a deferral of current pleasure because of the material success rat-race. On the contrary, there is theoretically no limit on what one might anticipate with pleasure. Nor is it true that the culmination of plans is always experienced in the abstract. This experiencing too can be direct and deeply felt.

Presumably a humanistic position should affirm the value of both kinds of experience. The awareness movement performs a service by stressing that often the worthwhile goal of satisfying the individual's felt needs has been subordinated to the dominant aims of "the system." But bear in mind that such needs are many and varied. They are direct and indirect, psychological and social, short-term and long-term. They range all the way from the physiologically based to the symbolic. It is inconceivable that they are all "here and now" needs. When you get right down to it, despite all the research and theorizing (anthropological, psychological, genetic, etc.), we do not really have a clear picture of the human being's "basic" (objective) needs. In seeking to enhance the individual's experience, a much better concept to work with would be that of options.

Maximizing options for all (including that of directly enjoying many types of experience) is necessary, if we really value the individual. Focusing exclusively on the intense experiencing of whatever options are now available can easily blind one to gross disparities in option availability. Of course, the expressed intent always is to widen the range of (experiential) options: to open up additional paths. But self-awareness specialists clearly prefer some paths to others. They are forever derogating the "old consciousness" (with its rationality and predictability). What they offer does not readily complement these qualities. More typically, it seeks to supplant them.

For the person whose "here and now" is appalling, and for whom a meaningful future is not discernible either, new modes of consciousness will not be enough. This is where present-centeredness really bogs down. Maximizing options in any meaningful sense requires social and political action. That means setting goals, planning, coordinating. (See Part Two of this book for various examples.) Self-styled visionaries like

Charles Reich and Theodore Roszak can blandly assert that
the new experiential outlooks will give rise to a better social
world. But that won't make it actually happen.

In his controversial best seller *The Greening of America*,
Reich proclaimed the imminence of "revolution by consciousness." Through a process never adequately spelled out, this
would remake our society, now that "structure and politics
have begun to seem utterly irrelevant." Once enough people
decide to live differently, to enjoy life rather than sacrificing
themselves to a worn-out system, "the political results will
follow naturally and easily, and the old political forms will
simply be swept away like immovable logs when the river
rises."[14] Well, we have yet to see it. Admittedly, there has
been some interesting small-scale experimentation—for example, the communes. Yet there is no evidence whatsoever
that the new outlooks are significantly undermining the
dominant social structures that shape our lives. Or that they
are about to do so. If living in the present is helping unloosen
any logs, it isn't replacing them with ones that are more useful.
And for most of us people, a sink or swim situation seems to
prevail, much as before.

Return to Childhood

The philosophy of here and now represents a withdrawal from
the inevitable complexities of adult existence, an attempt to
return to the relatively straightforward, often directly rewarding, life of a child. Awareness literature is replete with references to the special qualities of children—who for these
purposes are frequently grouped with lower animals and
"primitives." Children are said to be "natural." They act un-
inhibitedly, and with "simple grace." They still have their
innate capacity for joy, and reveal the basically human inclinations toward warmth and outgoingness. They are, in short, as
yet unsullied by restrictive social conditioning. To be sure,

there is an element of innocent naiveté in this depiction. Yet there is considerable truth in it as well. The question remains, however (even for those of us who favor changes in many current values and child-rearing patterns): Just how child-like can adulthood be made to be?

In a sense, traditional psychoanalysis can also be described as a return to childhood, though with the aim certainly of going well beyond. There, we seek insight into our early experiences in order to illuminate unresolved inner conflicts, to understand what may have interfered with a normal developmental process. But Freudians do not seek to reinstate the supposedly pure childlike feelings and behaviors. On the contrary, they are quite prepared to allow the individual certain controls over them, "defenses" against them. Some inhibitions, some degree of "inner control" are considered healthy, even essential. Indeed, when the Freudian patient reverts to the emotional context of childhood, he or she is likely to face the charge (diagnosis) of "regression."

Primal therapy is similar to Freudianism in focusing heavily on early life experiences. It urges, however, a quite different form of returning to childhood. This approach isn't much interested in producing insight. And it doesn't believe at all in "healthy defenses." Janov insists that adults are still, literally, experiencing those primal traumas. As a consequence, nothing will do but to overthrow them "by force and violence." Dealing with symbolic derivatives is "useless, and this is what has made psychoanalysis such an agonizing, drawnout affair." We need to go directly to the need and to the feeling. For Janov, most adults really are children (emotionally). This is what we must bring out into the open. And that's what the "primal" accomplishes: "Primal patients are not acting. They *are* the little children totally out of control."[15]

Most current awareness prescribers follow neither the Freudian insight model nor the Janovian violent-overthrow model. Insisting that we must deal directly with the present, they see both paths as counter-productive. Even psychoanalysts Mildred Newman and Bernard Berkowitz emphasize present-centeredness, in their fantastically successful best-selling *How to Be Your Own Best Friend:* "What others once did for you, you can now do for yourself. When you're thirty, you don't need your mother to love you the way she did when you were three. . . . That's all over; it's ancient history. You're your own man—or woman—now. But many people will not realize that."[16] If we focus on our immediate experience and become (now) fully and freely functioning individuals, emotional blocks that stem from our early years will dissolve or become irrelevant.

Childhood, in this view, is not primarily something we should each work through or reenact. Rather, it is the qualities of childhood in general that are esteemed. Children are described as living proof of self-regulation, and the naturalness of free-flowing behavior. They exhibit a sense of wonder over all aspects of their environment. They know how to play, and how to enjoy it. Above all, they are spontaneous; they are, as it's so often put, "in touch." Fritz Perls offers us a classic awareness statement: "If you are in the now, you can't be anxious, because the excitement flows immediately into ongoing spontaneous activity. If you are in the now, you are creative, you are inventive. If you have your senses ready, if you have your eyes and ears open, like every small child, you find a solution."[17]

Is it any surprise then that the awareness-makers prescribe childishness-reviving formulas? A good example is found in the "discovering one another" chapter of the relating guide, *Intimate Feedback*, referred to earlier. "Exercise 3: Sticky Fingers," aims at helping us "recapture the innocence of childhood" by eating a normal meal with our fingers. "Notice how revolting it first feels to plunge your hand into your gravy or fried egg, then see how quickly it does not seem to matter any more. Try feeling one another. Be aware of the different textures and temperatures. Talk about it with one another."[18] In

this as in other "exercises," the authors are deadly serious
about teaching us how to be natural. Spontaneity by the book,
so to speak.

Adulthood, according to such advisors, has become for the
most part an unnecessarily grim business. On the one hand,
adults have been restricted to an arbitrarily narrow range of
experience—conditioned to like it or assume it's the only
possibility. On the other hand, people have become jaded in
the sense of taking for granted—in effect, ignoring—the wonders of nature and of living. We have been brainwashed into
believing we must leave childlikeness behind. (The very term
"childishness" being, they would argue, a verbal smear.) Usually they declare "real maturity" to be an important life-enhancing quality. But they reject most conventional ideas about
what it means to be mature. This is a bit like their approach
to the concept of character. Real maturity means being fully
aware and free-functioning. What passes for maturity is all too
often automaton conformity, rigid future-focusing, a deadening deliberateness. True maturity incorporates the virtues of
childlikeness, and only when one is enslaved by a "false"
maturity does one try to surmount them.

Accompanying such ideas is a rather unique conception of
responsibility. This is a matter that will much occupy us
throughout this book. Its pertinence to the question of reviv-
ing childlikeness is pretty obvious. In large measure, responsibility is what separates children from adults. The child is
not held responsible for the consequences of his acts to the
same extent as adults. By the same token, the child's daily
existence is not hemmed-in by a burden of sobering and
weighty responsibilities. To the new ideologists, many of the
adult's so-called responsibilities appear to be a sham, a refusal
to face up to living in the present, a capitulation to the routinization of experience. But clearly, not all of us would agree.
In fact we might well insist that it is precisely and only because of not having to face up to adult responsibility that the
child can be so spontaneously and continuously "in touch."

Awareness statements on responsibility develop two main ideas. Both can be viewed as distorting and limiting. One of these themes is that nobody is responsible for us but ourselves. As we will see, this notion often is carried very far indeed. External (social) forces are not at all responsible for determining or shaping our lives. We must take responsibility not only for our acts and feelings, but also for what is done to us! And we are pretty much free to shape our lives as we ourselves see fit. Hence the new version of positive thinking (discussed in the next chapter), in which there are virtually no limits to what we can accomplish if we are only sufficiently "aware."

Just as we must take full responsibility for ourselves, so too must others. We cannot be responsible for them. Responsibility-through-a-sense-of-obligation prevents us from attending to our own needs. Desirable as it may be for each person to recognize and assert his or her own needs, the results of nobody taking any responsibility for anyone (or anything) could add up to wholesale irresponsibility. Under the best of conditions, we should indeed not have to be responsible for others. But not feeling responsible for or toward other people can easily degenerate into lack of interest in, or empathy for, others. As will be evident when we consider more closely the matter of relationships, this self-only-responsibility theme carries the seeds of a new manipulativism. This is just the sort of thing the self-awareness movement insists it will overcome.

The emphasis on taking charge of oneself does, of course, imply a situation different in important respects from that of the child. The child is not expected to (indeed cannot) tend to very many of his or her own needs. These new guidance specialists are saying that adults must become independent. But again, responsibility is only to oneself. Anything beyond that is burdensome obligation. Furthermore, the responsibility is to oneself in the here and now. It is to satisfy one's immediate needs. It is to refuse to defer gratification in the name of some future or abstract goal.

This may be independence, but at what cost? In several

ways, at the cost of relinquishing full adult responsibility. Such responsibility implies moving beyond or through independence toward interdependence. It implies mutually rewarding activity and shared outlooks. It implies responsibilities toward others and toward the society at large. These responsibilities often may be taken up voluntarily and without a consciousness of oppressive self-denial. What the advocates of self-awareness really want is to have things both ways. Spontaneity and community, self-interest and intimacy. Locating all forces and responsibilities within each individual, the new ideology (if its requirements are met) ensures a kind of return to childhood. For it is only the child-adult who cannot be held to any standards other than his or her own.

A Higher Consciousness?

How do we know when we are achieving self-awareness? One of the major signs is being able to experience unusual states of feeling. Most schemes for advancing self-awareness place some degree of emphasis on what Carlos Castaneda, in *The Teachings of Don Juan,* calls "nonordinary reality."[19] This is a helpful term, since it highlights the fact that what is sought is, indeed, out of the ordinary. For that is precisely the point. One cannot be fully aware in the feelings-context of the ordinary everyday world of living, because the range of accepted experience is too narrow. So we must enhance sensitivity, expand perception, heighten feeling. Certainly those are all potentially desirable goals. The problem lies in trying to incorporate these new states or abilities into a meaningful overall life scheme. Nonordinary, by definition, can never be ordinary.

Psychologist Robert Ornstein and others have noted that recent laboratory studies reveal two functionally specialized "sides of the brain." While the "left" hemisphere (found on the right side of the body) mainly governs analytic "linear"

thought, the right one "seems specialized for holistic menta-
tion." It is "more holistic and relational, and more simulta-
neous in its mode of operation." As I mentioned earlier, it is
this previously unrecognized, less intellectual and more intuitive mode, that many of the awareness exercises (such as
meditation, and other efforts to alter ordinary consciousness)
seek to release. The experience that results, according to Ornstein, is "outside the province of language and rationality,
being a mode of simultaneity, a dimension of consciousness
complementary to the ordered sequence of normal thought."[20]

This last comment suggests a special problem. Invariably,
these altered states of feeling are described as being "indescribable." Hence it becomes impossible to question their reality
(how does one refute a vision?), and also (even accepting
them as real) to rationally assess their meaning and value. For
the committed rationalist, this produces a real bind. On the
one hand, the awareness-heighteners insist that nobody who
has not experienced such states is qualified to comment on
them. Yet to the rationalist, reports by ecstatic participants
will hardly seem objective. The new experiencers, however,
argue that that's precisely what we suffer from—too much so-
called (and actually limiting) objectivity. From their standpoint objectivity is the problem, not the solution.

Actually it's not likely there are many informed people
around nowadays who would persist in disbelieving the widely
encountered reports of heightened sensory experience (especially through LSD and similar drugs). If for no other reason,
the ubiquitous smoking of marijuana has increased our
receptiveness to such accounts. Nonetheless, and especially
when these states are continuously said to be unanalyzable
and only capable of being hinted at through words, one really
doesn't know exactly what to make of them—other than
recognizing they can embody some extraordinary perceptions
and feelings.

Alan Watts, advocate of Zen Buddhism and other Eastern
disciplines, writes that "when you know for sure that your

separate ego is a fiction, you actually *feel* yourself *as* the whole process and pattern of life."[21] Some accounts claim that by a kind of negative implication, one senses also the inadequacies of ordinary social life. Thus, the editor of an anthology on LSD reports, of his own experience with the drug: "My exponentially heightened awareness saw *through* the static, one-dimensional, ego-constricted, false front which is the *consciousness*-contracted reality of the everyday world. This was no evasive flight *from*, but a deep probe *into* reality."[22]

It has even been claimed by some drug enthusiasts that LSD and similar "mind-blowers" enhance intellectual clarity. For example, Canadian writer Robert Hunter asserts: "The mind trains with drugs. It acquires new reflexes, a new kind of coordination. It exercises its muscles and gets itself ready to take the leap into the future."[23] A kind of better-thinking-through-chemistry, to paraphrase an early Dupont commercial. Something similar seems to be implied when Maharishi Mahesh Yogi and his followers label their approach to awareness-enhancing as the "Science of Creative Intelligence." Mostly, however, the claims focus on new kinds of feelings, and the putdown of normal intellect is pretty explicit. Tom Wolfe captured this well, in his chronicle *The Electric Kool-Aid Acid Test*: "But these are *words*, man! *And you couldn't put it into words.* The White Smocks liked to put it into words, like *hallucination* and *dissociative phenomena*. . . . The whole thing was . . . *the experience* . . . this certain indescribable *feeling*. . . . Indescribable, because words can only jog the memory, and if there is no memory of. . . ."[24]

We know from numerous accounts that the alterations of consciousness produced by such drugs heighten direct sensation. Pretty much the same seems true of most techniques for getting "high without drugs." As commentators on rock music —often cited as an important component of the new consciousness—like to emphasize, the appeal of "rock" lies in the feeling conveyed. The lyrics are strictly secondary. Whatever specific new feelings are sought, from the standpoint of ordinairly experienced reality they are otherworldly in nature.

That is, after all, what the esoteric disciplines of the East are all about. To be in the world, but not of it—as the Sufi tradition would have it. This otherworldliness, along with the focus on process rather than substance, makes very clear that the so-called new consciousness involves withdrawing from everyday life. External behavior is not important. Robert Ornstein notes that, "Both Zen and Sufism emphasize, as they do in the exercise of self-awareness, that one can do whatever one wishes as long as one is not attached to it."[25]

Perhaps the most dramatic depiction of new-consciousness withdrawal from conventional reality appears in R. D. Laing's *The Politics of Experience*, a book which has in common with Castaneda's writings an enormous appeal for youth in our society. Since our everyday existence seems, to this maverick British psychiatrist, so substantially insane, the very effort to distinguish between sanity and insanity is brought into question. True sanity requires abandoning the false self our alienating society imposes. What we have called breakdown into madness may actually be a kind of breakthrough. "It is potentially liberation and renewal as well as enslavement and existential death." It hardly comes as a surprise then that Laing should (in his ecstatic "Bird of Paradise" chapter) laud the attainment of schizophrenic-like states: "If I could turn you on, if I could drive you out of your wretched mind, if I could tell you I would let you know."[26]

Nonordinary states of consciousness are frequently described as being "higher." Even if we accept the notion of feeling high as appropriate to some situations, this general usage is most questionable. Given the desocialized and de-intellectualized consciousness that is involved, a term like "deeper consciousness" seems more accurate. Indeed, if we look at these new modes of sensing from a sociopolitical standpoint, they begin to look more like a "lower consciousness." At any rate, connotations of loftiness and superiority are quite unwarranted.

It may be correct to believe we have at times exaggerated the value of sheer intellect. Yet that is no basis for going over-board in the opposite direction. To cast aside not merely excessive rationality, but all rationality, would be simply a new kind of reductionist error. Perhaps most "new conscious-ness" advocates do not really want this to happen. Regardless, the difficulty remains that transcendence and nontranscen-dence coexist very uneasily, if at all. People who want ecstasy may not be able to have rationality in the same breath. And if ecstasy-seeking is part of a genuine repulsion against existing social forms, then it is quite unlikely to be accommodated within those dominant ways. Perhaps in part for these reasons, some spokesmen for a new awareness lower their sights a bit —from full "transcendence" to a more limited type of sensory exceptionalism.

Potential and Growth

In many self-awareness formulations major code words for success include "human potential," "personal growth," and "peak experience." None of these terms is defined with preci-sion. Yet all are treated as irrefutable goals, unassailable guidelines for individual improvement (if not also for social change). To question these notions has become akin to en-gaging in subversive activity. However, it is the awareness enthusiasts themselves, whose conversation is liberally sprinkled with references to potential and growth—to cover virtually anything and everything of which they approve—who are en-gaging in loose talk.

Quite a few of my earlier comments regarding "liberation" and "joy" apply here as well. In fact these terms, along with "awareness" itself, often are used more or less interchangeably with "growth" and "potential." As one becomes liberated to experiencing joy, one develops more self-awareness and hence comes closer to achieving one's full growth potential. Or, since the terms are used so loosely, we could just as easily turn this around. As one grows and achieves more of one's potential, a major consequence is self-awareness and joy. All these notions are used in an expansive, ever-optimistic manner. They are seen as facets of some underlying or all-enveloping organic process. In a vague way, horizons (for growth, etc.) are seen to be unlimited, yet the substantive paths real people may have to follow never seem to enter the picture.

As we have already seen, the new outlook assumes that because of stifled feelings human beings are failing to realize their full potential. But exactly what kind of potential is this? Here again we are dealing with an interiorized, content-neutral process. Potential and growth are thought of and talked about in strictly personal terms. Their presence or absence is determined in or through the individual's own feelings. Growing is a matter of developing general capacities. Potential to grow has little to do with the patterned aspects (structures, values, etc.) of *how* we live, but rather with the ways in which the individual *goes about the process* of living.

Thus there are (abstract, objectless) capacities to love, to be creative, to be in touch and spontaneous, to identify with others, to become autonomous. Never mind the uses to which such capacities might be put. The crucial thing is to develop them—and hence, grow. Developing our capacity potentials seems to be all that's needed to make us happier and the world a better place. This view obscures the fact one can use creative and autonomous capacities for bad purposes as well as for good. It seems to imply that as soon as people achieve their true potential for joy in living all bad purposes will simply disappear. To believe this requires disregarding objective clashes of interest, constraining social structures, in fact the entire patterned content-context within which personal capacities necessarily come into play.

Basically, then, the individual's true potential is a potential to feel. Objects and content are largely irrelevant. Indeed the awareness movement is so fixated on enhancing sensory sensitivities that "bad purposes" can only exist really in connection with non-feeling. Once one feels, fully and properly, one is by definition good. And since the individual can simply bypass the social order in seeking to achieve this kind of personal development (a point to which we'll return in the next chapter), there are virtually no limits on how far one can grow. Psychologist Abraham Maslow, one of the originators of the personal-growth approach, foresaw the advent of "the ideal, authentic, or perfect or godlike human being."[27] The Maharishi sees TM as producing a "state of eternal freedom," and unleashing "unlimited creative energy."[28] And Jerry Greenwald, typical of human-potential popularizers, proclaimed self-awareness (as we saw above) to be an "endlessly available opportunity."

One could go on to cite statement after statement from the recent self-exploration literature asserting the never-ending possibilities for human growth. The idea of continuous growth does have a certain value. It emphasizes that we are always changing. Perhaps this might encourage us not to be complacent. But, again, the perpetual stress on remaking the person (not the person-affecting situation) works against such a possibility. Typically, unlimited growth is presented as hampered only by our unnatural desire for security. As in the case of risking pain in order to reach joy, we must abandon our excessive security-consciousness so we can continuously grow. From this standpoint, almost all (personal) change seems good, and virtually all stability bad.

Suppose we believe that this is more often than not true, or at least that continuous change is inevitable? Even then, glossing over the substance of changes is confusing and disturbing. What changes? To what ends? Again, the awareness-makers want to have things both ways. (Indeed, that very tendency seems in some way built into the neutral-process idea itself.) They tell us that growth never stops, that a person is never too old (or weary, or poor, etc.) to develop. Yet they fail to warn us that we must distinguish between good growth and bad growth. For in a sense, all new experience represents change or growth. That hardly means that every such experience is desirable. If it did we would be unable to say there is ever any wrongdoing or unnecessary suffering in the world. The naive assumption in the new ideology is that once people begin to really grow, only good growth will occur.

Telling Americans that the potential for (favorable) personal growth is virtually unlimited, may feed a kind of dissatisfaction to which they already are prone. If we aren't changing enough, there must be something wrong with us. Such a conclusion focuses the dissatisfaction in the wrong direction. Emphasizing change at first sounds radical, but why should we conclude that the failure to achieve potential is a personal one? Under this approach, as Russell Jacoby has nicely expressed it, "the attention of the discontented is diverted from the source to the surface."[29] Preoccupation with personal growth masks the failure to confront directly the question of society's potential—on which individual growth so crucially depends.

Creativity

One of the more solid concepts associated with recent emphasis on potential is that of creativity. In his analysis of "peak experiences," Abraham Maslow concluded that some people are more "self-actualizing" than others, and that self-actualization is the path toward growth and human fulfillment. Maslow set forth (on the basis of many individuals' responses to inquiries about their "most wonderful experience or experiences . . . happiest moments, ecstatic moments, moments of rapture . . .") an array of values associated with peak experience, and qualities characteristic of self-actualizers.[30] (We'll come back to some of these when we see what he had to say about "relationships.") Crucial to both concepts is the stress on living creatively.

Creativity is more than just painting, writing poetry, or making music. It's an outlook on, or (better yet) a way of feeling about the whole of life. Again, the concept merges with others in the awareness arsenal. It's not clear whether creativity is synonymous with, causes, or is caused by being in touch, being aware, and functioning freely. (Of course, the new ideology insists that all distinctions are suspect!) All we are told is that it's essential to growth and authenticity. Through being creative we break the social mold and become real persons.

Predictably, this kind of creativity is felt to be closely tied up with the harmonious sensing of "organic unity" and with listening to those alleged inner voices that promote "self-regulation." For example, in the literature of gestalt therapy much is made of "creative adjustment"—which mostly seems to mean adequate "contacting" by the organism of its environment. Essentially, creativity seems but another term for describing the very process of exploring oneself and one's surroundings. Thus, Maslow depicts as a kind of primary creativity (that need not involve the production of specific works of creative art), "that which comes easily and without effort as a spontaneous expression of an integrated person, or a transient unifying within the person. It can only come if a person's depths are available to him, only if he is not afraid of his primary thought processes."

Discovering this generalized type of creativity came as a surprise to Maslow. Earlier, he had fallen into the trap of associating creativity with specific ("artistic") activities, and with the production of an "output" of creative works. Among his research subjects who disabused him of such notions were a poor and uneducated but "original, novel, ingenious, unexpected, inventive" mother, wife, and homemaker; a psychiatrist who was extremely "creative" in seeing each patient as a unique person; and a man who convinced him that "constructing a business organization could be a creative activity." As a result, Maslow came to distinguish between "special talent" creativeness and a type that in self-actualizing people "sprang much more directly from the personality" and showed up in various aspects of ordinary life. In this content-neutral notion of creativity, presumably any specific task might be performed creatively. The possibilities for political abuse of this amorphous conception (e.g., "creative warfare") should be apparent.

One of the things that distinguishes and identifies self-actualization (a term Maslow recognized might cause difficulty, and for which he suggested substituting the not much more specific "full-humanness") is a somewhat greater than usual ability to undergo "peak experiences." With this term, apparently Maslow meant to cover not only the various states of extreme transcendence, but also a wide range of exceptionally joyous, alive, "creative," and deeply felt experiences. Such experiences are ego-transcending, ends-in-themselves, more absolute, unified, and directly grasped than ordinary experience. And they are potentially disorienting (of the sense of time and space). People in these experiences tend to become "more integrated, more individual, more spontaneous, more expressive, more easy and effortless, more courageous, more powerful, etc."[31]

The peak experience seems to bear a special relation to creativity. So indeed does the entire self-awareness outlook. Returning to the conventional notion of creative activity (as in "creative arts"), this seems to be one of the few specific task-oriented fields in which the new ideology deservedly maintains a strong position. Here, thinking in awareness terms has in part resulted from—and yet also strongly reinforced and promoted—productive and meaningful experimentation in an area in which people actually work.

In the creative arts, the intuitive mode of consciousness is of the very essence. For the most part, artistic experience does not thrive on antiseptic intellectuality and pre-planned orderliness. On the contrary, creating art requires being imaginatively immersed in and receptive to a flux of unfolding experience. This is not to say that the artist does not ever plan, organize, or have substantive ideas. However, some of the major self-awareness themes do seem to be crucially important for working in the arts. Artists must have or develop a perceptual and experiential openness. They need an exploratory and innovative spirit that will enable them, at least on occasion, to transcend the routines of normal life and develop a unified and emotionally compelling image. Art is a uniquely expressive endeavor. Only secondarily does it have instrumental value.

We can see then why there would be many direct and indirect links between the creative arts and the movement for self-awareness. Movement spokesmen often hold out the creative artist as a model of free and healthy functioning. They see our response to an art work as a prototype of holistic experience. It is not simply by coincidence that the term centering refers both to a major technique in the art of pottery and a frequently encountered self-awareness concept.[32] Often this word is used as roughly synonymous with "aware" or "together." The main idea it conveys is detaching oneself from external influences and becoming "focused" (another word having artistic connections—as in photography) on oneself. Centering also fits in well with such notions as self-regulation and here-and-now. It seems to be both a technique for, and the accomplishment of, true awareness. According to Fritz Perls, "achieving the center, being grounded in one's self, is about the highest state a human being can achieve."[33]

Traditionally, there has been a close connection between the esoteric disciplines of the East and a wide variety of art forms—ranging from Haiku poetry and flower arranging to the various exercise modes (so popular now in this country) which often seem more akin to dance than to ordinary calisthenics. Another long-standing link between the arts and efforts to enhance awareness has been the use of consciousness-expanding drugs by major literary figures (Poe, Baudelaire, De Quincey, Cocteau; and more recently such writers as

Aldous Huxley, William Burroughs, and Allen Ginsberg).
Huxley, in particular, has become a kind of indirect awareness
guru, through his personal account of experience with mesca-
line, "The Doors of Perception."[34]

In the performing arts, expressivist themes are especially
pronounced. Training of actors and dancers has always emphasized self-awareness, body consciousness, and a fluid expression of the emotions. Recently, the tie-in with the awareness
movement in this country has become quite explicit. We now
have "primal theater workshops" for actors, and "creative
body movement" centers that meld together dance and
growth training. Techniques popularized through encounter
groups—such as "psychodrama" (a therapeutically aimed acting out of a real-life or hypothetical situation) and "role-playing" (a similar if less elaborate device, in which often one
plays the role of another person)—have probably contributed
to this blurring of the line between performance training and
therapy.

Avant-garde theater and dance in America today have been
drawing heavily on self-awareness concepts and techniques.
Playwright-critic Arthur Sainer describes, in *The Radical
Theatre Notebook*, a "radical loosening" that has occurred in
contemporary American drama. To a large extent, this has
involved a new "presentness" of the performer, an effort to
offer not just ideas about experience but experience itself,
directly. (On the fringes between performing and studio arts,
the spontaneous and unpredictable "happening" comes to
mind as a form that displays particularly close affinities to the
new self-awareness outlook.) In addition, a conviction grew
that, "New body movements, new sounds, a new awareness
must be formed in order to make comprehensible [the] underground life of the race."

Avant-garde theater ensembles began also to make direct
use of encounter-group and associated techniques. Sainer
notes that "trust exercises" are "now traditional with ensembles." And emphasis began to be placed on breaking down the

barriers of feeling between actors and audience. Describing
the Performance Group's landmark audience-participation
production of "Dionysus in 69" (performed in a garage in the
Soho district of Lower Manhattan), Sainer notes that, "The
performance had a sense of free-flow to it, as well as being
sensuously physical, improvisatory, ritualistic. The spectator
had the sense that he could help make the production, he was
encouraged to get into the play, to participate in the rituals,
to chant, march, touch, strip and be fondled." Characterizing
more generally the impact of some of these avant-garde theater experiments, Sainer comments that, "we move into the
essential area of simply seeing and feeling, we lose the power
and the need to judge, we can't ask of it because we're caught
up in answering it. And what it asks of us is not to see it but
to see ourselves."[35]

Much the same kind of thing has been happening in modern dance. As might be expected, here some of the explicitly
body-conscious awareness schemes (such as those of Lowen
discussed above) have a special pertinence. A West Coast
dancer, Anna Halprin, has led the way in seeking to combine
training and performance with personal growth. Using
"growth" workshops as a central part of dance training, seeking to minimize in performance the dancers' separation from
an audience, she has actively promoted the dance as a vehicle
for the fullest possible self-expression. Taking her dancing
into synagogues, prisons, schoolrooms, and onto streets and
beaches, her expressed aim is the unification of art and life.
According to a recent account, "She believes art should be a
means of healing our society, of making it more humanistic,
of rediscovering spiritual values, of making the mundane
creative."[36]

This attempt indicates the reciprocal nature of the relation
between self-awareness and work in the arts. Just as awareness
is thought to enhance creativity, exposure to creative fields of
activity may also increase self-awareness. Thus creativity "facilitators" see working with art materials as a good way for

people to "find out what they are feeling inside themselves."
The writer of this statement, who runs art-experience sessions
for a variety of people seeking "increased self-awareness, enjoyment, or spontaneity," often is asked what the point of the
sessions is. Are they intended to be therapy, or art work, or
childish games? "My answer is that we are doing all of these.
The activities or products may seem chaotic and meaningless,
but they are related to the philosophy that knowing for one's
self on the perceptual level is the most valid kind of knowing."[37]

In a rather different context, we find a strong interpenetra-
tion of art and everyday life in rock music. Such music,
Charles Reich even argued, "has become the deepest means
of communication and expression for an entire culture."[38]
Here again, the relation of rock to the search for awareness is
a reciprocal one. It is an important part of the counterculture
which, as I noted earlier, helped generate the new self-exploration. At the same time, a new sensitizing to self (and especially body) helps explain rock's enormous appeal. Expanding
awareness has borne a close relation to much popular music
—improvisation and the widespread use of drugs by jazz musi-
cians illustrate this. But rock has been extraordinarily productive of culture heroes, and indeed has at least reinforced an
entire subculture. A great deal of its impact is in the rhythm,
in the "vibes." According to one ecstatic assessment, "It pole-
vaults the wall of conceptualization and explodes among the
machineries of perception, seldom directly affecting the way
we think, but almost always affecting our rhythm, which may
prove to be the key to those reflexes which go into the making
of feelings, and, in turn, responses, attitudes, biases, selections,
all the subconscious interactions which at their extreme pole
crystallize in thought."[39]

The idea of reducing thought to rhythm suggests the issue
of "creativitizing" all of life. Without doubt it is a good thing
to encourage people to be creative, to engage in all kinds of
activities and confront diverse life challenges with a creative

vitality and a creative flair. But such efforts should not be allowed to divert our attention from other, at least equally important goals. A task performed creatively should be more satisfying and no less effectively accomplished than one that is not. For those in a position to concentrate on creative flair, nothing much can be lost in doing so. At the same time, however, mere creativity (as my earlier ironic reference to creative warfare should make clear) does not ensure desirability. And for many purposes, creative flair is patently not enough. To the extent they don't realize this, the new ideologists encourage social myopia. Enhancing life by approaching it creatively is most worthwhile. Trying to reduce life to the exercise of some abstract creative capacity is absurd. The awareness movement sometimes seems torn between urging a new "art of living," and asserting itself as a "science of growth" (to use Claudio Naranjo's term). It's not clear whether or how it can manage at the same time to be both—art and science. Unless these complex aims are clarified or tempered, it could drift meaninglessly in a hazy area between the two goals.

III

Learning To Be Real

Roles and Selves

How does one become a really authentic person? We would all like to know. Though its precise meaning is never adequately specified (by now we should expect this), "authenticity" is another cult word of the awareness movement. It involves bypassing prescribed social roles and being our real selves. We are authentic when we "take charge of" ourselves, when our choices and reactions flow spontaneously from our deepest needs, when our behavior and expressed feelings reflect our personal wholeness. So runs the standard awareness litany.

This general formula cuts across various specific schemes, even if each has its particular way of stating it. In gestalt-oriented circles it is said that, "Maturation is the development from environmental support to self-support." For Alan Watts, "when a man no longer confuses himself with the definition of

himself that others have given him, he is at once universal and
unique." And in their recent manual *Shifting Gears*, the
O'Neills stress the importance of "giving up your mentors."
There comes a time, "when we are ready to give them up,
break free and become ourselves. We go beyond their belief
in us to a belief in ourselves . . . [this] means that you have
learned the ropes sufficiently so that you can manage your own
life."[1]

Social conformity is seen as the major impediment to being
authentic. Typical is Charles Reich's characterization of the
old-consciousness person, as having a "lack of wholeness, because of his enforced playing of roles and subjection to outside
standards . . . no inner reality against which to test what the
outside world tells him is real."[2] Others present more "internal" analyses of inauthenticity. Thus, body-emphasizers such
as Lowen stress the physical manifestations (and body-related
causes) of uncertain identity. Arthur Janov (as we might
predict) sees the unreal self as a defense against those "primal
feelings" deeply implanted during early childhood. Another
variant of this internal emphasis is found in Eric Berne's
transactional analysis—given renewed popularity through
Thomas Harris', *I'm OK—You're OK*. There, the role-playing that occurs (in the form of various catchily designated
"games") is similarly taken to reflect conceptions of self and
of others derived from the early years. Especially significant
is the "You're OK—I'm not OK" outlook, which this theory
claims is a frequent outcome of the child's early experience
with his or her parents.[3]

Almost all the new awareness specialists argue that a great
deal of the time people are not being their real selves. Also
that (in one way or another) "roles" are to blame. Here again,
they are propagating some highly misleading ideas. Is there
such a thing as a person's "real" self? And why must role
always be treated as some kind of dirty word? With respect to
both of these matters, we are now being fed a great deal of
unfounded and distorted interpretation.

Authenticity, in this conception, means self-regulation. Nice

as that might be, it just doesn't jibe with what we know about
the real workings of the social world. Our extremely diverse
life activities occur as part of this world, not in spite of it. They
inevitably reflect more than what any inner-guidance mechanisms (however holistic) could provide. Writers on self-
awareness usually recognize the reality of events and forces in
the "external" world. However, their subjectivist leanings push
them into seeing this context as being only secondary in importance. As a result, they advance a vague and optimistic
notion of the individual's true (inner) self, and a very narrow
and excessively negative conception of social role.

Each of us wants to know "the true ME." Indeed, personal
identity has become a significant (middle-class) preoccupation in this "age of analysis." But in a sense psychoanalysis and
psychiatry have done us a disservice on this score. Undoubtedly they have directly helped a lot of people to deal with
identity problems. At the same time, they have fostered a
kind of general identity consciousness which itself can be a
self-fulfilling prophecy. In some circles it has become almost
obligatory to experience identity crises and for people to believe they are out of touch with their real selves. A corollary
is the very belief that there is such a thing as a real self or
true identity. Today psychological self-help popularizations
reflect and reinforce this questionable belief (epitomized in
the title "Be the Person You Were Meant to Be"). They offer
short-cut formulas for achieving this much sought-after state.

Why do I say that it's misleading to talk about a person's
real self? The social psychological literature on self and identity is voluminous. Obviously, I cannot explore it adequately in
this brief discussion.[4] But for our purposes here, no elaborate
analysis is really necessary. A few straightforward sociological
observations should suffice. For the sociologist, a person's self-
conceptions (and the self-images he or she would like to project to others) invariably reflect that person's accumulating
experience in social interaction. Gradually and cumulatively
built into this system, yet always in some degree changing,

are the effects of myriad actions on our part, responses by other people, and our counterresponses.

If the notion of real self refers to all that we have incorporated through these interactive processes, then it may have some meaning. The composite effects of these processes are reflected in our ongoing behavior and outlooks. In this sense, we do bring to each new situation something that is uniquely our own. But to the awareness mentality such a formulation seems too mundane. Something deeper, even more basic to the whole person, is required. We're never really told what it is exactly, or where it is to be found. Somehow it emerges spontaneously from the essential needs of the particular individual. Since this approach does not seem to stress genetic influences, the elusive something appears to be rather mystical —a kind of inner personal spirit. There is nothing wrong with asserting strongly the personal worth and integrity of each individual. But this view goes way beyond that, to an exaggerated claim regarding the individual's intrinsic uniqueness. As such, it defies both proof and refutation.

If there is such a thing as the real self, then presumably it's also possible to *not* be oneself. When, if ever, does this happen? Usually when we say, "Oh, I'm not myself today," we simply mean that we are not feeling very well, that we wish we were not acting the way we are, or that we don't want to be held fully accountable for our mood or behavior. Theories about unreal selves may have some value in the domain of psychopathology, but their extension into everyday life does not make very much sense. We might speak of multiple selves, or self-components, or the composite kind of self I've already described. However, the possibility of being not yourself at all implies a unitary, stable essence that no amount of authenticity-imploring is going to pin down. (In a way such a stable inner core almost seems to contradict the notions of openness, expressivity, and continuous growth that dominate awareness thinking.) The plain fact of the matter is that we are always our selves, because what else could we be.

When I praise my children, when I am irritable with my wife, when I do a piece of work well or badly, when I smile more than usual or less than usual, when I feel physically exhilarated or glum, when I unexpectedly experience joy or attain a much desired goal—there really is no meaningful way of describing any one of these as being more than any other a reflection of my self. Of course it's possible that for a given person one behavior, mood, or attitude is more characteristic than another. Yet nobody is arguing that statistical frequency or consistency is what indicates the true self. No matter how much I might like to feel that only my preferred qualities are my true ones, there is no evidence or reasonable argument to support such a belief.

This misinterpretation of self is tied up with equally unhelpful ideas about role. The two are seen as being diametrically opposed. Roles, it is maintained, go a long way toward explaining why the individual is unable to assert his or her real self. In this usage, "role" means "role-playing" (consciously manipulative simulation or mindless conformity). For the sociologist, the idea of role connotes much more than that. It designates the patterning of behavior, the clusters of rights and obligations associated with specific positions in the social order. It helps us to understand how people can manage everyday interaction without falling into total confusion. As my reference to rights and obligations suggests, roles are not just restrictive—they are facilitative as well. Through our various roles we maintain links in elaborate networks of interaction. In fact, it is through roles that we develop, express, and maintain the self.

In their usual fashion, awareness zealots are highly selective in the examples they use. The roles they usually talk about represent a few highly restrictive, conservative patterns. Thus, they are greatly exercised about the businessman role associated with monetary-success striving. Or the narrow housewife role that has been imposed on women. Or the jingoistic superpatriot role. They fail to see that roles are everywhere.

The serene craftsman, the loving mother, the Buddhist monk—all these too are filling or playing social roles. So are the "creativity facilitator," and even the person we might label an "awareness freak." Being social implies a high probability of displaying behavior and outlooks held in common with other individuals in similar positions or situations. Only the absolute hermit can (perhaps) avoid roles entirely. We may try to lose the self in meditation, or to express ourselves with total spontaneity in an encounter group. Nonetheless, there is a "right way" to go about meditating, and a pattern of appropriate behavior for encounterists. However much we may proclaim ourselves open, these are social as well as personal situations. It is perfectly natural that they should display regularities, much as other social situations do.

Americans do not easily accept the fact that roles are inevitable. Our indoctrination with an ethos of individualism encourages us to resist it. Hence we are quite ready to believe that there are only two alternatives: a totally unsatisfying rigid conformity or a spontaneously free-flowing choice of our unique individual ways. As is so often the case, the motivation underlying awareness statements on self and role is commendable. But the absence of social analysis, one might say of social awareness, leaves these formulations shortsighted and unrealistic.

One of the major aims is to overcome the powerful emphasis on status-striving, on competition for social prestige. A central idea of the human-potential movement has been that we are not primarily occupants of specific social positions, rather we are all simply human beings. The difficulty with this is that while we are indeed human beings, we are most definitely not *simply* that. Each of us shares with others membership in certain social groups and categories that may have considerable relevance to our sense of identity. We hold (in common with others) particular kinds of jobs, we share systems of beliefs and preferences, we occupy on the basis of various criteria places in the broader social system. We may be pleased with and proud of these social positions of ours, or we may seek to change them. Or we may wish to radically change the system of which they are parts. But we cannot ignore them, and they will not just go away. From this standpoint, status-striving involves more than inauthentic individuals. It is built right into our social system. Changing it, or any other entrenched part of the system (see Part Two) requires much more than individual self-exploration and change.

Playing down invidious distinctions, and emphasizing our common humanity, certainly can help to eradicate stereotypes and reduce prejudice. However, as we'll see when we consider implications of self-awareness for particular segments of our population, focusing exclusively on our "human" capacities may not at all be the most radical kind of awareness. On the contrary, the effective surmounting of differences often may first require that we acknowledge and assert them. The false belief that social positions and roles are completely dispensable places extreme limits on what it means to be "aware."

The Return of Positive Thinking

This lack of social perspective is strikingly apparent in the self-help theme that permeates recent self-awareness programs and writings. As we have seen, concepts like self-regulation and human potential suggest that every person has limitless possibilities to change, grow, and experience joy. Combine with these notions the idea that we have nobody and nothing to blame for our troubles but ourselves. You end up with a doctrine that neatly sustains our culture's traditional insistence that the individual should be self-reliant.

We seem endlessly susceptible to popularizations of this theme. Hence the many widely read volumes that tell us (among other things) how to stay healthy, stay thin, achieve financial success, grow old gracefully, divorce happily, deal with our children, enjoy sex, and make the most of singledom, or married life; as well as how to repair furniture and minimize our income taxes. In many respects, the most popular awareness books are self-improvement manuals conveying much the same do-it-yourself spirit. Through jacket copy and advertising each one proclaims itself to be the ultimate in the self-help genre. Through numbered formulas, or grossly simplistic assertions, they offer instant guidance to creativity, spontaneity, and joyful living.

According to Mildred Newman and Bernard Berkowitz (*How to Be Your Own Best Friend*), "the kingdom is in us; we already have the key. It's as if we're waiting for permission to start living fully." Blaming someone or something outside of ourselves is easier, they argue, than facing up to taking the actions needed if we are to defeat our unhappiness. "If you decide you want to help yourself, you can choose to do the things that make you feel good about yourself instead of the things that make you feel terrible."[5] In *Be the Person You Were Meant to Be*, Jerry Greenwald similarly condemns blaming. He cites as one of the signs of "nourishing" living, being able to answer this question affirmatively: "Do I experience my conflicts and 'problems' as essentially of my own making?"[6] The new awareness tracts, then, take up where clergyman-writer Norman Vincent Peale left off in the 1950s —with such works as *The Power of Positive Thinking*.

Peale purported to "demonstrate that you do not need to be defeated by anything, that you can have peace of mind, improved health, and a never-ceasing flow of energy. In short, that your life can be full of joy and satisfaction." Citing Emerson on self-reliance and other stalwarts of Americana, Peale went on to describe many cases in which individuals he knew had overcome obstacles, and to set forth amazingly neat formulas to help others follow in their footsteps. Thus we find, "ten simple, workable rules for overcoming inadequacy attitudes and learning to practice faith," "seven practical steps for changing your mental attitudes from negative to positive, for releasing new thoughts, and for shifting from error patterns to truth patterns," and "ten practical rules for getting the esteem of others." These lists (along with others—such as rules for effective praying) are said to embody tested and proven methods. They are given indirect endorsement through Peale's constant references to successful businessmen, prominent citizens, etc. for whom they worked. In the last analysis, according to Peale, "the basic reason a person fails to live a creative and successful life is because of error within himself."[7]

It is striking that the current awareness writers, who would like to see themselves in the vanguard of some revolutionary new consciousness, end up sounding so much like the author of this "greatest inspirational best seller of our time." This similarity goes well beyond a shared philosophy of self-reliance. The "listing" tendency is another common feature. Often, in the recent books, this takes the form of matching columns of Do's and Don'ts. Nena and George O'Neill, in *Shifting Gears*, provide a ten-point "crisis-solving set," ten suggestions for "successful decision-making," and "seven keys to creative self-management." Their earlier blockbuster, *Open Marriage*, was similarly geared to lists, especially "eight cardinal guidelines to aid you" in achieving the open marriage goal. Greenwald's *Be the Person You Were Meant to Be* presents a checklist of twenty-seven items through which readers can determine for themselves the extent to which their outlooks and behavior are "nourishing" or "toxic." Usually these same writers, somewhere in their work, express disdain for pat formulas. Frequently, they state that there are no shortcuts to self-awareness, that one has to work for it. But apparently once you're on the self-help habit, the associated formula-making tendency is equally hard to kick.

Again much in the manner of Peale, we often find in these recent books success stories involving influential or well-to-do persons. The characteristic title-dropping and social-class selectivity are seen in a list of Americans from "all walks of

life" said to now be engaging in transcendental meditation:
"astronauts, senators, congressmen, a high-ranking China
expert, Strategic Air Command personnel, Pentagon generals,
a famous dietician, Wall Street brokers, New York Jets foot-
ball players, UCLA Bruins basketball champions, Broadway
playwrights, members of an eminent repertory theater, scientists, artists, businessmen, professors, doctors, teachers,
housewives, students, and children."[8] Supposedly these reci-
tals are meant to show that anyone (even the already successful) might benefit from the technique. But the attempt
to use celebrity appeal to generate new customers and the
accompanying success-through-association theme are evident.
An array of show-business figures provides back-cover testi-
monials for one leading psych-help book. A Transcendental
Meditation Society uses poster endorsements by leading ath-
letes (including—ironically, in the light of alleged serenity
goals—some from body-contact sports).

To an extent, then, the popularization of awareness is but
another version of the quasi-religious dogma of optimistic
individualism that has always sold so well in America. It
appeals almost exclusively to the middle and upper classes, it
is politically innocuous and socially complacent, and it is
being promoted and marketed in the best Madison Avenue
tradition. It has become the new civic religion of the United
States. The kind of empty religiosity theologian Will Herberg
once aptly described—"a religiousness without religion, a religiousness with almost any kind of content or none. . . ."[9] Yet
we know that this religion of the self has its peculiar rituals,
produces converts, and (as we are seeing) requires members
to accept much on faith. What it is not likely to do, however,
is inculcate any moral code of deep substance or galvanize the
individual into meaningful social action of any sort.

To these new awareness preachers, the concept of a "social
gospel" (in which a religiously charged social consciousness
motivates efforts to ameliorate social ills) is anathema. True,
they frequently note that oppressive social conditions make it

difficult for us to experience our real selves. But far from trying to change these conditions, we should accept or at least ignore them. One of Greenwald's guidelines for so-called nourishing living would have us give up our "attempts to control the world and accept life as it is." It is hardly surprising that among patterns of "self-induced toxicity" he includes "rebellionitis" (involving "fantasies of oppression," and constituting an "elaborately disguised scheme to escape the self").[10]

Just as rational thought is seen as a deflection of real impulse, blaming the "system" is treated as a kind of passive and whining evasion of the need to help ourselves. It is all right to blame another individual directly for not letting you meet your own needs, but finding fault with broader social conditions diverts attention from the main task. These writers rarely distinguish between realistic and nonrealistic blaming. (This is at least consistent, for their content-free approach makes the basis for blaming irrelevant.) Nor do they show interest in the possibility that blaming the social system itself will spur decisive efforts to change it. Ultimately, according to the new self-help writers (and as we've seen they're quite explicit about it), if you're unhappy you have only yourself to blame.

This conclusion fits in well with the movement's peculiar approach to responsibility. As we saw, it would hold us responsible for what happens to us, as well as for the actions we ourselves take. Many of the "new therapies" make a great deal of this matter of personal responsibility. Focusing on the present, they constantly urge the individual to take charge of himself or herself. Albert Ellis's "rational-emotive therapy" (which seeks to combine rational assessment with the new expressiveness, and which also is heavily influenced by Alfred Adler's "inferiority complex" theories) is one example. Here the element of rationality implies that we should realistically acknowledge limits on what we can expect to accomplish by ourselves. However, we still create our own disturbances by failing to limit our expectations. According to Ellis, his clients learn "that *nothing* is truly awful, terrible, or horrible; that he can *never* be rated as worthless (nor as being great); and that *no* human can legitimately be condemned for anything he does."[11] Another version, in other words, of helping one-self by looking on the bright side.

William Glasser, in his "reality therapy," gives another twist to the responsibility theme. Glasser believes our difficulties (personal and social) stem from our unwillingness to place blame. At least Glasser adopts the conventional meaning of responsibility. People should be held responsible for the predictable consequences of their acts. But he is prepared to apply this notion so broadly and loosely that we end up being responsible for everything. He states, for example, that "we must never delude ourselves into wrongly concluding that unhappiness led to the patient's behavior, that a delinquent child broke the law because he was miserable, and that therefore our job is to make him happy. He broke the law not because he was angry or bored, but because he was irresponsible. The unhappiness is not a cause but a companion to his ir-responsible behavior."[12]

What we might find to be a reasonable conclusion in specific instances is thus elevated into a general moral diagnosis without any supporting evidence. For these new therapists, as for most self-awareness promoters, we are simply deluding ourselves when we point the finger at the allegedly social and institutionalized sources of individual behavior and unhappiness. One way or another, the focus must be kept on the unique person, on his or her special capacities and self-induced failures. It is only because we don't maintain this focus that broader social forces can begin to hold sway. Thus, the O'Neills state, "If you do not manage yourself, then by default either circumstances or other people will manage you."[13]

The new self-help statements disregard almost entirely the social context within which people act. They glibly ignore social roles, the requirements of which inevitably affect the extent to which and ways in which we can help ourselves. Perhaps I should emphasize again that this is true of roles we want to play, as well as of those we may consider oppressive. Even roles we enjoy occupying intersect in ways that require us frequently to accommodate one to the other. And self-help writings most glaringly neglect the impact of the socioeconomic class system on our abilities to manage life situations (see further discussion at end of this chapter).

The combination of general awareness themes and self-help urgings produces a mixed message—part unending optimism, part self-blame and resignation. We should have confidence in our self-regulatory capacities and trust our basic impulses to lead us in the right directions. If we do so, our potential for vital living is great indeed. Our power to achieve this, however, is a two-edged sword. On the one hand, we can control our destinies. At the same time, to be out of control means to have personally failed in some way. The self-help message encourages those who are succeeding to feel good about themselves. It is much less satisfying for those who are not.

They are being told, essentially, to accept what life has to offer—and to enjoy it. Here the no-joy-without-pain concept is brought into play to "cool out" the potentially discontented. Newman and Berkowitz assert: "Life is not a picnic—or a rose garden. The world is not run for our benefit. There is no escaping the human condition, which involves pain and difficulty and loss. But we can bring everything we have to bear on the challenges life presents and make the very most of what it offers us. If we liberate ourselves from our fantasies and learn where our real resources lie, a whole world is waiting to be explored."[14] For people who have ample resources besides those of the "internal" variety, this may be fine. Individuals who are lacking in this regard may not be so sanguine.

My Needs, My Deeds

"Hell," says one of the characters in Sartre's play *No Exit*, "is other people." To those who counsel the new awareness, hell is having other people decide for us how we should think, feel, and behave. It is being excessively compliant, always accommodating the wishes or expectations of others, and therefore never getting around to satisfying our own needs. This is one of the ways, we are now informed, in which we create our own unhappiness. Again, it is we ourselves who have the solution. We must stop putting ourselves down. We must stick up for our (interpersonal) rights. If we're not on our own side, who will be? Conscious self-assertion is the order of the day.

Somehow the conscious self-asserting now being urged on us seems at odds with the hoped-for free functioning that would flow spontaneously from our inner impulses. Yet as we just saw, asserting the self is a major theme in the popular awareness literature. It is built into the notion of responsibility as "taking charge of oneself." In these current psychological-help manuals, we are constantly being implored to take the initiative, to make our own decisions, to determine for ourselves how we shall live. We should, they insist, fight the tendency to engage in apologetics, and simply "be." Justifying and explaining are tip-offs that we are being regulated by others. Meeting our deeply felt needs requires no external justification.

The stress on self-assertion ties in well with the antipathy to roles and role-playing. Roles are abhorred because, in this conception, they involve taking behavioral cues from other people, not following those inner voices. Just as they isolate the self from all social context, the new awareness prescribers argue that self-esteem should not depend on other people. "It is up to us to give ourselves recognition," say Newman and Berkowitz.[15] We will have favorable conceptions of ourselves when we are truly aware, self-regulating, satisfying our real needs. Just how this will occur in the absence of reinforcing positive reaction from the people around us is not at all clear. Since the self is built up out of an accumulation of responses and counterresponses, this belief in some kind of self-activating self-esteem must be an illusion.

Both this approach to self-esteem, and the idea that being

is its own justification, reflect the tendency to ignore the content of life situations. Neither the substance of our behavior, nor its actual or likely consequences, seems very important. There is no recognition that we may develop self-esteem because of substantive *accomplishments,* even perhaps because of things we have done *for* other people. Or that it is perfectly natural for us to model ourselves after those we admire and to seek their approval. (The guru–disciple pattern so prevalent in self-awareness circles hardly signifies that this allegedly unnatural tendency is being surmounted!) Or that we may rationally evaluate ourselves in terms of shared standards that represent something more than just emanations of our particular inner selves.

Self-esteem becomes a matter of *feeling good about* (or even *in*) oneself, rather than of *thinking well of* oneself. Indeed, it seems to be reduced to feeling good, period. We find a similarly distorting repudiation of rationality and standards in the insistence that we do not have to justify or explain ourselves. Since the only true guides to natural and proper behavior are internal, there is never any basis for external judging. Here too, it is not what one does that counts, but how one does it (whether one is "centered," guided by one's own needs, etc.). If we can validly claim we are self-regulating, then—presumably—anything goes.

Despite the apparent contradiction between free-flowing inner guidance and systematic planning to consciously push our personal needs, training in self-assertiveness is the latest movement fad. Commenting on the first of the recent assertiveness-training best sellers and in anticipation of more to come, *The New York Times Book Review* suggested that the approach might well become "the reigning parlor self-therapy." The book, it pointed out, "follows the basic rules for success in the genre: (1) keep it simple and practical, don't induce any unsettling introspection; (2) be positive (life is full of problems but they can all be solved); and (3) touch a nerve—in this case, one supposes, a sense of being pushed around and low self-esteem that is abroad."[16]

The Times was exceedingly accurate in spotting this incipient trend. In just the few months since its prognostication, the competition for the self-assertion market has become so intense that another such volume now carries, tucked around its regular book jacket, a special streamer describing it as "The #1 Assertiveness Training Book!" The streamer features an endorsing blurb from none other than George O'Neill, co-author of *Open Marriage* and *Shifting Gears*.[17] Full-page ads for this volume's predecessor and major sales competitor proclaim "the behavior therapy that's sweeping the country— SYSTEMATIC ASSERTIVE THERAPY—the most useful and successful technique ever developed to turn the tables on the everyday manipulators in *your* life."[18]

As the reference to "behavior therapy" may suggest, the idea of specific training in assertiveness stems from a somewhat different theoretical and research tradition than many of the new schemes. It does not share the typically negative view of social conditioning. On the contrary, this approach is based on psychological theories that see conditioning as the basis of most behavior, and reconditioning as a major therapeutic technique. Here, the idea is that we exhibit a conditioned response to acquiesce in situations not of our own choosing, to unhealthily defer to the wishes of others. If we put our minds to it, we can recondition ourselves to place our own needs first. Nothing succeeds like success. Once we have begun to experience the satisfactions of self-assertion, the tendency to slight our own basic desires will fall by the wayside.

According to the assertiveness theory, we often are conditioned to passivity through a fear of being disliked or rejected. And there is a kind of passivity spiral. Such inhibitions on behavior increase our feelings of self-doubt and dissatisfaction. This in turn restricts our actions still further.[19] The reconditioning process involves reversing that spiral. If we practice actively asserting ourselves, this will lead to a reduction in our self-doubt and passivity. And that will enable us in the future to act more freely to meet our own needs.

The new assertiveness books recommend a variety of "behavior assignments" in which the trainee consciously and unapologetically makes demands on other people. For example: "Go to a newstand where you are not known, take out a five-dollar bill, and ask for a fifteen-cent newspaper. Do this twice the first week. The second week try it with ten dollars. Make your request matter-of-fact. Do not apologize." Or, "Go into three stores. In each, try on an article of clothing . . . but buy nothing. This gives you the freedom to say no. If you see something you really want to purchase, go back later."[20] The possibilities for creating exercises to further such training are more or less unlimited. They include forcing oneself to do tasks one has been too timid to undertake, telling close relatives and friends what you "really" think of them, calling public officials to complain vigorously about this or that state of affairs. The point in all this is not really to get people to accede to your demands. Rather, simply to get yourself to where you're able to voice them.

Assuming a low enough frequency of serious backfire, it probably is true that doing this sort of thing enough will make a person more assertive. Whether that necessarily is a good thing is, of course, another question. We will return to this issue shortly, in considering recent ideas about "relationships" (next chapter). Assertiveness-trainers do recognize the pitfalls and are eager to assure us that the dangers are slight. They insist that our efforts to overcome other people's manipulation of us will not merely result in our manipulating others. They seek (though with uncertain clarity) to distinguish between (appropriate) assertion and (inappropriate) aggression. According to one leading assertiveness manual, "You have the right to maintain your dignity by being properly assertive—even if it hurts someone else—as long as your motive is assertive, not aggressive."[21] Though the same authors go on to admit that there are "certain borderline cases in interpersonal relations where the rights aren't clear," this claim that good intentions can in effect justify harmful consequences will not be reassuring to anyone on the receiving end of such asserting.

As I've already noted, assertiveness training does, to some
extent, acknowledge the importance of rationality and show a
concern for specific human purposes and projects. A great
deal of attention is paid to determining goals (albeit individual rather than collective ones) and evaluating success in
achieving them. There is also a heavy emphasis on decision
making. And the idea of self-concept is given at least a close
to normal meaning. Even though self-esteem should be self-
generated (and not sought through external approval), it is
recognized that this quality is built up through successful
actions. For the assertiveness specialists, doing is as important
as just being. Satisfying one's needs, in this treatment, comes
close to being a matter of advancing one's (individual) interests, achieving one's goals.

Because of this more rational tinge, training in assertiveness
may have considerable value in overcoming some of the effects
of social subordination. So far, the best example of this has
been the use of such training among women. Women's confidence and ability to stand up for themselves have been
stunted through cultural stereotyping, childhood socialization
for passivity, and restricted role-options. Obviously, learning
to be assertive won't by itself correct all these institutionalized
facets of sexism (see Chapter V), but as a coping device, and
(on a large scale) an initiator of change, assertiveness may
prove to be of great importance. Thus the codirector of a
women's workshop on "Asserting Yourself in Jobs and Personal Relationships" recently noted: "Assertiveness has always
been so difficult for women, but now work is becoming the
center of women's existence just as it has been for men. . . .
Women must learn these techniques. They can't maintain
the gains they've made without fighting for their jobs. But
at the same time I'm concerned about avoiding ruthlessness
in favor of cleverness and restraint. My motto is 'I will not
cheat thee, but I will out-smart thee.' "[22]

Despite its goal-oriented and other rational qualities, assertiveness training continues to have much in common with
other efforts to enhance self-awareness. There is the same

stress placed on open expression of feelings—perhaps particularly, in this case, negative ones. Direct and honest communication, and willingness to reveal oneself, are highly valued. There is even a biophysiological rationale for this approach. Lowen presents a kind of psychophysiological analysis of the word "no." According to him the person who is unable to say "no," does not really "know" who he or she is or what he or she wants.[23] Assertiveness trainers may have such formulations in mind when they include in their programs exercises that focus on body movement, vigorously physical expression of feelings, and nonverbal communication.

Although it pays some attention to specific situations, overall assertiveness training perpetuates the content-neutral idea. What is being taught is thought of as a content-free interpersonal skill that could be used in most any context. Again, it is individuals who are deficient and require change. The new therapists like to see themselves as opposing all forms of "adjustment" psychology. Presumably they want to free people to go their own ways, and not simply to conform to the existing social arrangements. Yet when it gets down to taking remedial action, they seize upon the individual person. In this scheme, all that's wrong with the patients is that they are inhibited and passive. They need to learn to stand up for themselves. But new fangled or not, their self-appointed helpers are, by and large, therapists. They are used to seeking (and finding) the sources of unhappiness within the individual. That society might be the "patient" rarely enters their minds.

What's Missing?

Self-awareness specialists insist they can teach us how to be real. In this overview of their basic concepts, we've already looked at some of the reasons why this claim is questionable. Part Two of the book deals with more specific applications of their approach. We will see, in additional detail, how it fails to come to grips with the complex problems people face in their actual life situations. At this point, however, it may be useful to summarize briefly and develop just a bit more the grounds for criticism that we've thus far uncovered.

As I've already suggested, the new mentality incorporates a limited and highly distorted conception of what it means to be real. This distortion and limitation amounts to nothing less than a neglect of the substance or content of life. People seem to live, in this view, in a social vacuum. They need meaningful ties to other human beings. But somehow they can develop these quite apart from (and without the support of) a surrounding context of specific social institutions and forms. They can do this, and satisfy their other basic needs, just by being themselves. And this is defined mainly in a negative way—through the absence of "role-playing." By developing a variety of content-free expressive and interpersonal skills, they will unleash their natural spontaneity and creativity, and thus experience "growth."

With the partial exception of assertiveness training, the overwhelming emphasis is on being, not doing. The idea that a person is what he or she does, is abhorrent to most self-awareness promoters. It is the very process of self-expression and of experiencing oneself (in some abstract manner) that counts, not the specific activities involved or the consequences of one's actions. The self develops largely without reference to goals, projects, and standards. This (hypothetical) individual is capable of a quite unreal degree of autonomy, and of achieving virtually all life satisfactions in some yet-to-be-explained solitary and internal way.

What this boils down to is a repudiation of culture—in the broadest sense of the term. To the sociologist or anthropologist, culture means a great deal more than works of art. It refers to the entire fabric of learned, shared, and transmitted patterns and themes that permeate a society. As such it includes not only a great many tangible objects produced in the society, but also intellectual productions and systems of social norms (standards of approved behavior) and values. The importance of this lies not so much in any society-wide cultural consensus, as in the central role culture (in general) plays in shaping social relations. It certainly is not the case that everybody in a given society agrees on all norms and values. There may indeed be significant variations in this regard. Sometimes these may reflect more or less cohesive subcultures within the larger system. But, one way or another, and whether in consensus or conflict, people cannot get along without culture. It is the meat of social existence. In fact (as case studies of children kept in almost total isolation demonstrate), a person without culture is barely human.

Now, of course, the awareness counselors never say they favor abolishing culture. They simply don't take it into account in depicting the development and uses of a person's self. By implying that people can express themselves adequately in a kind of culture-free way, they push moral relativism to a shaky extreme. Since what you do is not important, but rather how you go about doing it, any cultural content must be as good as any other. And they reduce human beings to the lowest common denominator. By ignoring sociocultural content and its variations and concentrating on people's "natural" impulses (with emphasis on biophysiology and lower-animal analogies), they slight almost all that is truly distinctive of humans.

It is true that the movement stresses one cultural item—the value or goal of personal pleasure. Without question, this is a valid goal. But awareness enthusiasts come close to seeing it as the only goal, and—as we saw—to define it almost exclusively in sensory terms. What I called social joy—pleasure less as a result of conscious pleasure-seeking than as a by-product of other social activities—rarely enters into this depiction. We might indeed be better off increasing our concern for direct pleasure, and reducing our domination by monetary-success and status-striving goals. Yet, important as sensory pleasure may be, it is difficult to imagine a viable collective way of life built around this single theme.

Just as the awareness movement makes short shrift of culture, so too does it glibly dismiss most of the realities of social
structure. My earlier comments concerning the concept of
social role pointed up part of this gap in the new ideology.
Perhaps the most flagrant distortion involves the socioeconomic class system. From what one could tell by looking at
most of the awareness literature, there simply is no such thing
as social class. The problems considered and case studies presented are almost entirely oriented to middle- and upper-class
living conditions. Yet little or no mention is made of this,
and broad principles are advanced that supposedly apply to
all "humans" everywhere.

A striking example of this is *Shifting Gears*, authored by
two anthropologists.[24] No doubt the O'Neills are accepting of
broad cultural differences, and also are prepared to view with
equanimity certain variations in personal life style. Yet somehow, the significance of socioeconomic differentials within
our society seems to have passed them by entirely. Thus they
can write, presumably with straight faces, about "the option
glut" (our world today is "a veritable kaleidoscope of options")—a concept they or anybody else would have a hard
time explaining to the unemployed or the disenfranchised.
Similarly, they can discuss "the guarantee myth" (the belief
that financial and social security will produce happiness—
which then results in disillusionment) without it ever occurring to them there are people among us who never came close
to anticipating such security for themselves in the first place.

In much the same way, the O'Neills take an incredibly
ethnocentric view of personal crisis, apparently based on their
own middle-class values and experience. Of course they assert
—in characteristic self-awareness fashion—that the specific
nature of a crisis is not as important as "our *attitude* toward
it." Nonetheless, there are crises and crises, and those they
choose to discuss are, at least arguably, trivial. For example,
in discussing variations in "crisis potential," they report: "In
Latin America the loss of a maid for some middle-class women
is a real crisis. . . . On the other hand, for a young

American career woman who is constantly juggling the immediacies of household, job, and children, the loss of a maid is only one of a series of problems to be dealt with." (Needless to say, it never occurs to the O'Neills to discuss what a maid's crises might be like!)

Again, when they write about people's varying resources for meeting crises, all they mean by this is emotional resources. That economic resources might help a person confront a crisis, or avoid it to begin with, seems quite outside their range of comprehension. This is what comes of focusing too heavily on self-awareness. You become virtually unaware of the real world around you. And so it goes throughout this strange book. In support of their general propositions about maturity, coping, and the attainment of real security, the O'Neills cite case after case of characteristically middle-class situations. Thus, we are asked to consider whether the middle-aged, college-educated housewife should now take up a career; whether the successful businessman should switch to a more creative line of work; whether the failed would-be actress should look elsewhere for achievement and happiness. Of course, it is quite permissible to write exclusively about the middle class if one wants to (though, even then, this soap opera-like treatment would probably be inadequate). But one should say so. As far as I can recall, the O'Neills provide no such qualification. To imply, as they do, that they are grappling with basic human predicaments in ways that have wide applicability is most misleading indeed.

For the sociologist, the most significant fact about social class has to do not with prestige hierarchies and differences in life style (though they very definitely do exist), but rather with the distribution of "life chances." Study after study documents the extent to which in our society all kinds of chances in life—the chance to grow up healthy and to get good medical treatment, the chance for a good education, a decent job, and an adequate income, and the chance in turn for one's own children to have these opportunities—are strongly affected by one's initial position in the socioeconomic order.[25] Many of those comfortably located well up the economic ladder, and some others who hope to get there, refuse to accept as fact this phenomenon of differential life chances. Having been brought up on so many Horatio Alger rags-to-riches stories, we Americans still like to think it is all up to the individual.

With its interiorizing focus, and its insistence on personal responsibility, awareness thinking encourages and reinforces this naive individualism. It tells us of the endlessly available opportunities for joy through self-awareness. This might be all very well, if the more mundane requisites for happiness already had been met equally for everyone. But we know this is most decidedly not the case. While the American class system is a relatively open and free one, some of us are considerably freer than others to take advantage of these or any other opportunities.

I have already alluded to the marketing of awareness, and the fact that entering one of the commercial growth programs may be an expensive proposition. Of course, it is true that the awareness message also is being disseminated now at low cost through the psychological self-help books. Presumably these are accessible to everybody, though it is hard to imagine they could really have much appeal for poor people or the otherwise socially disadvantaged. If they do, it must be an appeal geared to complacent acceptance of their lot, to quietly making the best of things. Certainly, it's conceivable that even a poor person might feel somewhat better as a result of some of the new self-realization techniques. But, at best, such happiness would tend to be short-lived. Seduced into interiorizing their problems, the poor would only be diverted from the more urgent task of advancing their real collective interests.

This is another feature or consequence of social structure that the self-awareness outlook badly obscures. One would never think, from the awareness literature, that people share (on economic, social, or ideological grounds) common inter-

ests and goals. That it is natural for them to collectively favor
and seek to bring about or retain particular sets of social arrangements. That certain values are more important to them
than others. Again, such shared interests and values and the
actions that are linked with them represent a great deal of
what social life is all about. These collective elements are extremely important if we are to understand fully why people
act as they do, and how social institutions get changed, or
else (because of vested interests) resist change.

Most of the new awareness writers are silent on all these
vital matters. The idea of society as an arena for the broad
interplay of collective interests and values falls quite outside
the personal (and occasionally, interpersonal) focus they characteristically adopt. If they have any image of the larger society
at all, it seems to be one of a system that will be in harmonious equilibrium once the individuals in it are self-regulating. In this view, the realities of social conflict (and hence of
social change) are imperceptible. One attends exclusively to
the sensory responses and "internal guidance" of allegedly
unique individuals.

In the preoccupation with "process" (and lack of interest
in specific social forms), we are never told in detail what kind
of society would maximize even the possibilities for meaningful self-realization. There is, of course, the usual reference
to our presently inhibiting and restricting social conditions,
along with abstract proclamations favoring love, community,
trust, honesty, and the like. But what specific social arrangements would make these things possible? And how are we to
attain them? For many of the awareness writers, one hardly
gathers that it makes much difference.

This is not true of those self-awareness advocates who consciously align themselves with the counterculture. They do
have a vision of the good society. It centers around decentral-
ization and debureaucratization, repudiation of conventional
success goals and prestige hierarchies, protection of the natural
environment, communitarian living and economic arrange-

ments, and reassertion of individual craftsmanship. According to Theodore Roszak, "we should undertake to repeal urban-industrialism as the world's dominant style of life." The city and industry, "should exist in a supporting role and be strictly subordinated to the general pattern of life. They should be options and possibilities . . . but not the dominant mode." Super-industry should be leveled down "in favor of humanly scaled, labor-intensive alternatives."[26]

Just how are we to accomplish this? After all, the "repeal" of urban-industrialism is no small matter. While the awareness-oriented counterculturists at least appreciate the importance of social context, their ideas about how to alter it are extremely fuzzy. They simply assert (with practically no supporting evidence) that the allegedly new consciousness among individuals will produce strikingly new social forms. As we saw earlier, Roszak counts heavily on the unleashing of our "visionary powers." Charles Reich, in support of the same kinds of social arrangements, similarly asserts a totally new kind of revolution—"revolution by consciousness." These writers, disenchanted over the failure of traditional political actions to solve the world's problems, thus seek to reverse the classic position of Karl Marx, who stated: "It is not the consciousness of men that determines their being, but, on the contrary, their social being determines their consciousness."[27]

However, they do not provide, nor indeed could they, solid support for their new approach. In typical awareness fashion, they simply assert it. It's the individual that really counts, and that's that. Reich maintains that "consciousness is capable of changing and of destroying the Corporate State, without violence, without seizure of political power, without overthrow of any existing group of people." Further, that "culture controls the economic and political machine, not vice versa," and hence "social change, instead of beginning at the palace, comes up from below." According to him, Marx failed to realize the extent to which noneconomic concerns would dominate people's lives: "There is no class struggle; today there is only one class. In Marx's terms, we are all the proletariat, and there is no longer any ruling class except the machine itself."[28]

It can certainly be questioned whether even these most socially conscious of awareness touters have an adequate conception of social reality. In common with more run-of-the-mill awareness-makers, they have a ceaseless fascination with the direct experiencing of experience; and an incredible optimism about the potentialities of this process. They keep telling us that as the new awareness spreads (and more and more people "drop out" to lead different kinds of lives) radically new social institutions will emerge. But, as I've already emphasized, this doesn't really seem to be happening—at least not on any substantial scale. And for the segments of our population that are systematically oppressed, and want to do something about that now, this self-designated "vision" must in any case seem awfully remote.

Actually, most of the things currently done in the name of self-awareness have little if anything to do with social visions of any sort. Quite likely the average growth-center customer gives little attention to these issues, and knows nothing of these particular utopian formulations. The same is true, we can assume, of the typical reader of the modern self-improvement manuals. Awareness managers would have us keep things that way. As far as they're concerned, social consciousness only tends to deflect people from the true path. However, social reality is not about to evaporate simply through being ignored by these new specialists in interiorizing. Collective interests and grievances will not just disappear. Nor indeed will even our smaller-scale interpersonal problems evaporate in the wake of these oversimplifications. A look now at existing and proposed applications of the awareness approach—in specific life situations and problem areas—will make it quite clear that this is so.

Part Two / APPLICATIONS AND ABUSES

IV/ The Mystique of Relating

In Search of the Loving Person

"Together" people "relate well." A standard self-awareness formula. But does it really mean anything? Among the numerous debasements of English usage that we can ascribe to the awareness movement, this is one of the most unfortunate. Well-intended efforts to imbue a common word with heightened meaning end up producing a catchy but quite nebulous rubric. A model awareness cliché, "relating" is now applied to anything and everything. As a consequence its real usefulness all but disappears.

"Relating" is more than what occurs in specifiable long-term interpersonal relationships, meaningful or otherwise. It is a generalized skill that a person either has or doesn't have; one which can be taught and developed through appropriate techniques. If you have it, you can apply it in all manner of situations, not only in dealing with other people, but also as a response to objects, ideas, and even abstract causes. Nowadays we are likely to hear not only "She really relates," but also "I don't relate to Marxism." On at least one occasion, a graduate student responded during an oral examination: "I'm sorry, but I'm afraid I don't relate to that question."

This amorphous relating concept is grounded in the twin awareness emphases on expressing and communicating. It also reflects the conviction that substance-less skills will enable us better to "manage" life, and that there are simple, effective methods for learning them. Focusing on these supposed skills, on relating as an abstract process, those who would advise us never seem to ask certain questions that one might ordinarily expect to be important. Relating to whom? About what? And to what end? They insist that these issues are secondary. Ability to relate, the qualities one brings to all one's specific relationships—these are the heart of the matter.

Some of the concern with relating does represent a reaction against the loss of intimacy in modern urban society. Spokesmen for a youth-oriented counterculture, in particular, have emphasized the need to repudiate interpersonal competition and reassert a sense of community. Real intimacy, they have argued, requires breaking through the impersonality and fragmentation people experience in urban and bureaucratic settings. Thus the 1962 Port Huron statement of Students for a Democratic Society (often cited as a key manifesto of the New Left), included these words: "We regard men as infinitely precious and possessed of unfulfilled capacities for reason, freedom, and love. . . . We oppose the depersonalization that reduces human beings to the status of things. . . . Loneliness, estrangement, isolation describe the vast distance between man and man today. These dominant tendencies cannot be overcome by better personnel management, nor by improved gadgets, but only when a love of man overcomes the idolatrous worship of things by man."[1]

Current statements on relating bring together various ideas

of the counterculturists and the encounter-gestalt specialists. We must not allow our relationships to be dominated by role-playing, or to be instrumental (manipulative, exploitative) rather than expressive. Getting more "tuned in" will smooth out many of the difficulties we have dealing with other people. According to Philip Slater, in *The Pursuit of Loneliness,* "Because we have cut off so much communication with each other we keep bumping into each other, and thus a higher and higher percentage of our interpersonal contacts are abrasive." Regardless of the pressures of urbanism, we cannot allow ourselves to settle for segmentalized relationships. Thus Slater asserts, in a more recent book, that "partial involvement means partial fulfillment: A person who is never more than fragmentarily in the here-and-now is only minimally alive."[2]

Relationships must become less routinized and more spontaneous, less restricted by uptightness and more openly expressive of the individuals who are relating. People want to be loving and cooperative. An unnatural set of repressive social conditions has made them otherwise. Yet the self-awareness solution is to improve the individuals rather than change the conditions. The new relating advisors provide another illustration of the conversion of social discontent to personal inadequacy.

Encounterists offer both verbal and nonverbal exercises expressly designed to enhance relating. When group members, for example, publicly state the good feelings they have about each other, or when they hug, stroke, and cradle each other, this is supposed to free them up to giving and receiving affection more openly.[3] Trainers in body movement and body consciousness claim to relax tensions and overcome inhibitions that hamper freely flowing spontaneous relating. The relationships of "post-primal" patients are, according to Janov, exemplary: "They do not make unreal demands on one another because they are not unreal. Each partner becomes a viable human being, content to live and let live."[4] Advocates of meditation and other alterations of ordinary consciousness believe such techniques may undercut our tendencies to categorize and stereotype.[5] If that is so, our relationships may improve as we become able to focus on and respond to the uniqueness and wholeness of each other person.

The self-awareness approach to relationships has been especially influenced by the work of Abraham Maslow. In his book, *Toward a Psychology of Being*, Maslow emphasizes how important it is for each person to be treated as an individual. Human beings, he claims, exhibit a healthy resistance to being "rubricized" (categorized). Good relationships will reflect the fullness of perception and mutuality of regard that develop in purest form among "self-actualizing" people. Such people attain "being-cognition" (B-cognition, for short)—a mode of experience that is nonevaluating and noncategorizing, richly absorbing, and valued for its own sake. This contrasts with D-cognition—a partial, less fulfilling, classifying, and mainly instrumental mode organized to meet the individual's own "deficiency needs." Correspondingly, Maslow developed a distinction between "B-love (love for the Being of another person, unneeding love, unselfish love) and D-love (deficiency-love, love need, selfish love)." B-love is nonpossessive and intrinsically gratifying. B-lovers are "more independent of each other, more autonomous, less jealous or threatened, less needful, more individual, more disinterested, but also simultaneously more eager to help the other toward self-actualization, more proud of his triumphs, more altruistic, generous and fostering."[6]

In other words, more perfect. Few would argue with the desirability of these traits. The problem has always been getting people to act this way in real life. Authors of the new psychological well-being tracts are undaunted by this challenge. It is easy, once one is familiar with the basics of awareness doctrine, to anticipate the standard treatment they give to relationships. Turn to almost any general book on self-awareness, and you'll find a section or a chapter on good and bad relating. By and large, they all say about the same thing.

Openness and honesty are good. Relating according to someone else's rules is bad. Relating to the whole person is good.
Blaming the partner for one's own unhappiness is bad. Body-
and-feelings consciousness helps in relating. Repressing emotions doesn't. The relationship should be experienced for its
own sake, in the here and now. Letting it become too future-
oriented is deadly. Mutuality is the key to growth. Individual
"power plays" by the partners undermine relationships and
in the long-run rarely pay off.

Since the awareness movement has so heavily concentrated
its focus on the individual and his or her direct interactions,
one would think that at least on this topic of interpersonal
relations it would have some useful things to tell us. But even
here, it asserts potentially contradictory themes (for example,
independence and mutuality), makes glib assumptions about
the wonders of honesty and openness (implying that you can
"communicate away" almost any problem), and myopically assumes that a relationship can exist in abstraction from any
wider social context or meaning. While it is useful to emphasize that we are "people who need people," the movement
courts unreality when it acts as though relating occurs in some
kind of enclosed emotional arena. The self-contradictory feature of relating-through-awareness is implicit in the recognition (by awareness specialists Nena and George O'Neill) of
"a delicate balance between our self-assertiveness and our
caring that can be maintained only by respecting the integrity
of the other."[7]

Open Marriage and its Enemies

A good way to begin looking at major aspects of this problem
is to consider the O'Neills' *Open Marriage*, together with
some arguments that have been raised in criticism of their
position. This book combines teachings of the awareness
movement with some of the arguments of women's liberation.

It is at times rather moderate in its stance, most notably in insisting that the institution of marriage is still viable, and indeed valuable. In other respects, it is exceedingly radical—as when the authors claim that extramarital affairs need not imperil the marriage relationship. Much of the authors' indictment of traditional marriage patterns is useful. So are some of their prescriptions for change. Others, however, are advanced in the vague, unsupported, and glibly optimistic manner so typical of self-awareness popularizations.

As we have already seen, the O'Neills are very big on relating in the here and now. In particular they view this as an antidote to orienting relationships around the eventual attainment of security (financial and emotional). No amount of material success, they emphasize, can be expected to produce a mutually fulfilling relationship in the absence of the partners' personal growth. (Predictably, they give scant attention to the limitations on such growth produced by *lack* of material security.) The key to a successful marriage relationship is a commitment to the right of each partner to grow within it. Traditional (closed) marriage is unsatisfying precisely because it has not been built around this commitment. Once we open marriage up to this idea of mutual growth, each partner will be free to experience self-realization, and the relationship itself will be the stronger for it.

The O'Neills are optimistic about the possibilities for "synergetic growth"—in which the changes experienced by the individual partners would add up to an even greater beneficial change in the overall relationship. Closed marriage they see as static; open marriage as dynamic. Continuous change is the key to successful relating. "With change, new constellations of behavior, new ways of relating, new knowledge of the self, and an increased dynamism of interaction between the two become possible."[8] Little do they concern themselves with the fact that problems as well as possibilities may be created by change, or with the difficulty of maintaining a reasonable sense of continuity and security in the wake of such perpetual change. Nor are they reluctant (though they disavow any claim to "major formulas") about offering "guidelines" for this new kind of marriage relation.

In addition to the nowness theme, these guidelines pretty much boil down to openness and honesty, equality between partners, and role flexibility. They are designed "to help you develop competence and skill" in relating to a mate. To facilitate this personal-improvement process, the authors suggest a variety of awareness-related techniques—involving self-disclosure, getting and giving feedback, developing alertness to nonverbal communication, openness in family fighting, and the like. Along with these devices (aimed primarily at improving communication) they urge conscious efforts to understand the need for and to enhance role equality. For this purpose, they advise such exercises as role reversal (in which the partners role play each other's situation), or even more ambitious ventures in actual occupational exchange. As additional prerequisites for growth they emphasize the need of each partner for some time alone ("psychic space") and for opportunities to develop friendships (as well as to engage in activities) outside the relationship.

Have the O'Neills succeeded in telling us how to remake a major social institution through improvement in personal functioning? I think not. They do manage to advance some humane and helpful ideas. On one level, where they state the values they would like to see develop in marriage, it seems difficult to fault their argument. This is why the criticism leveled by George Gilder—in his provocative attack on the women's movement, *Sexual Suicide*—is largely misdirected. Unless one wishes to turn the clock back (as Gilder quite apparently does) to some ostensibly benign traditional marriage scheme, it is pretty hard to oppose such values as mutuality and equality. Gilder manages to do this only by resurrecting what is by now a heavily discredited notion of the naturalness of "sex-specific functions and responsibilities." The "real agenda" of open marriage, he insists, is "to reduce women to the condition of men, abjectly dependent on external performance and achievement."[9]

This statement is revealing, because at heart Gilder does not think women are equal. He thinks they're superior. Women have great power over men who are psychologically dependent on them. Only women can bear children. And only women can infuse relationships with those qualities of warmth and lovingness that now more than ever are so badly needed. Man, with his (inherently!) aggressive and competitive orientation, would for this purpose be hopeless. While the essential female role has changed somewhat, "its essence is the same. The woman assumes charge of what may be described as the domestic values of the community; its moral, aesthetic, religious, nurturant, social, and sexual concerns. In these values consist the ultimate goals of human life: all those matters that we consider of such supreme importance that we do not ascribe a financial worth to them." Though man's basic role is also indispensable, it is "relatively fungible and derivative. He is in charge of the instrumental realm: the world of work and the marketplace. Here, individuality is much less in demand."[10]

It is extremely difficult to square these contentions with the cross-cultural evidence showing variations in sex-role differentiation, the numerous recent studies documenting the impact of childhood socialization patterns on the adult outlooks and behaviors of the sexes, and our clear knowledge that neither sex has a monopoly on the capacity to perform any of these functions (save childbearing) successfully. There is considerable evidence also supporting the O'Neills' argument that much of the dissatisfaction with marriage has been due to the restrictions it has placed on equality of opportunity and mutuality of development (in awareness terms, growth).[11] Gilder's main critique actually centers on the O'Neills' strongest points. Of course, since *Sexual Suicide* is about women's liberation, it is not surprising that Gilder attacks *Open Marriage* as a manifestation of that movement. This is of a piece with the rest of his discussion—with includes (rather remarkably) criticism of day-care centers, of female competition for "men's" jobs, even of ending sex segregation in school athletics.

The O'Neills deserve strong criticism, but on other grounds. As my summary of their position makes clear, the idea of open marriage rests crucially on amorphous self-awareness themes and devices. What they want to achieve in marriage may (in the main) be praiseworthy. Their view as to how this can be done is much too narrow and simplistic. Gilder does touch on some of the relevant problems. For example, he properly charges them with "total incomprehension of what marriage is, beyond the immediate interactions of the two partners. One has no sense of the institution's role . . . of its location within a specific economy and society."[12] Yet, as one might expect, for him the main importance of this lies in their failure to see a need for role "complementarity," and to recognize that there simply aren't enough good jobs (outside the home) to go around.

A much more telling criticism might center on the O'Neills' naive faith in our power to produce significant social change through "mutual growth." If the windmills they're tilting at are the right ones, their weapons are not adequate to the task. We will return (in the next chapter) to the general question of how the new concern about awareness fits in with the women's movement. Although the two movements may in some ways have reinforced each other, self-awareness outlooks and techniques represent at best a small first step toward achieving the major goals of feminism. This is necessarily so, because the problems confronting women are so numerous, so interconnected, and so deeply institutionalized in the dominant values and the structure of our society. They are not simply a consequence of individual wrong thinking or personal malfunctioning.

For marriage partners or others to adopt such goals as mutuality and openness, or to practice "role reversal" and train themselves in "feedback," may improve their relationships.

But such activity will not by itself bring about real equality. That would require a social restructuring of opportunities, a provision of social supports that can only come about on a large scale through alterations in existing public policy. Equal access of the sexes to good jobs, equal pay for equal work, adequate and inexpensive day-care facilities, full control over unwanted childbearing, maternity and paternity leaves, and so on—in *addition to* changes in attitudes among both women *and* men. The O'Neills scarcely begin to hint at such needs, so caught up are they in the self-awareness ideology. They completely ignore the possibility that the deficiencies are systemic, not individual. And their almost total unawareness of social class constraints feeds this short-sighted view. Fixated as they are on middle-class situations and problems, it's quite natural for them to believe that better communication and mutual expressiveness will make people happy *and* reconstruct relationships. If you have enough money, you can always pay someone to take care of the kids.

Also strikingly absent from the O'Neills' book is any grain of realism regarding so-called nonpossessive relating. This is a standard notion in the awareness movement, emphasized by Perls, Maslow, and other self-realization gurus. We are not responsible for (or, it seems, to) other people. We should never try to "own" them. As the often-quoted "Gestalt Prayer" has it, "I do my thing, and you do your thing. I am not in this world to live up to your expectations. And you are not in this world to live up to mine. . . ."[13] The idea that we should never allow our personal identity to be overwhelmed by or submerged in that of another seems a healthy one. But the O'Neills, who argue for a close-to-absolute freedom for relating partners, and at the same time insist on the surpassing power of trust, carry the theme of nonpossessiveness to a ridiculously naive extreme. Gilder refers to "wish fulfillment" and he is right. As usual, awareness thinking intimates that we can have everything all at once.

Jealousy, according to the O'Neills, is not natural. We are

jealous when we are insecure in ourselves and in our relationships. Though jealousy and possessiveness undoubtedly do
at times impair relationships, it hardly follows that "sexual
fidelity is the false god of closed marriage." According to the
O'Neills, if your commitment is to your partner's (and hence,
your mutual) growth, sexual affairs outside the relationship
may be "rewarding and beneficial."[14] Just as honesty, openness, and trust will allow both partners simultaneously and
harmoniously to meet their own needs, so too will such qualities render potentially competing involvements innocuous.
This is perhaps a happy concept, but unfortunately wishing
for it will not make it so.

Awareness-oriented "relating" advisors believe in independence—emotional independence. They stress psychological,
not economic, self-sufficiency. While this girding up of
people's emotional resources is often a good thing, it can also
backfire. This is one of the dilemmas we began to sense in
looking at some of the self-assertiveness theories. If we become fiercely independent, making sure always to put our
own side first, will we at the same time be able to sustain
mutually fulfilling relationships with other people? Fortu-
nately, realization of these difficulties probably will deter most
of us from casually attempting sexually open marriages or
other extreme experiments in relating. As a sociologist special-
izing in alternative life styles recently noted (in a discussion
of group marriage and group sex), "Hitherto privatized, nu-
clear-family cultures do not lend themselves easily to such an
adaptation; our sense of possessiveness with spouses and jealousy still bulk in the way of such solutions. Perhaps another
generation, reared without sexism and jealousy, will adapt
better to such a form, but the numbers are few who can make
it work well today."[15]

But even less extreme forms of trying to maximize individual satisfactions may cause us problems. A heightened
sexual competitiveness could (as Gilder stresses particularly
well in his recent book, *Naked Nomads*) imply isolation and

frustration rather than freedom and joyous liberation—"men and women lost in the sexual shuffle and relegated to the singles game, in which almost no one wins."[16] On such matters, the self-awareness message is ambiguous. There is much talk about not exploiting other people. In Maslow's terms, we should cherish the other person for his or her Being. Relationships undertaken for instrumental purposes will be incomplete and unsatisfying. At the same time, there is even more talk about not letting other people exploit us. This is the whole point of assertiveness training, the popularity of which is quite striking. Can the hitherto manipulated avoid turning into the new manipulators? At present we don't really know. Self-awareness popularizers seem to believe it's possible. However, some of the actual behavior patterns their work is encouraging should cause us to be wary, if not downright alarmed.

To Learn the Relating Game

Many people in our complex kind of society more and more feel themselves to be at sea. Adrift in a confusion, if not always of options (as the O'Neills seem to believe) then at least of stimuli: "cultural noise" as well as literal noise. In large measure the appeal of popular awareness manuals may lie in their seeming to provide simple and optimistic "handles" that the individual can grasp in the midst of all this confusion. Yet the mixed message of the mass literature on relating could well leave people even more confused or dissatisfied than before. This is particularly true when self-help themes are amplified into a pragmatic strategy-guide for "winning" in one's relationships.

Contributing to the tendency for relationship-advising to move in this direction have been some of the ideas of "transactional analysis," first popularized by psychiatrist Eric Berne, in *Games People Play*. According to Berne, individuals attempt to deal with their "stimulus-hunger" and "recognition-hunger" by receiving and giving "strokes" (which can be psychological as well as directly physical). Stroke-exchanges (transactions) comprise for Berne the basic units of social interaction. To a considerable extent, these transactions are influenced by the "ego states" of Child, Parent, Adult—recapitulations of our earlier experiences, particularly as children with our parents—that, in varying degrees, we all carry around inside us. When one is dominated by the Parent, one behaves as the real parent would have done, and so on. Transactional analysis sees these ego states not as roles but as "psychological realities."[17]

Berne's concept of games is of greater interest for our purposes here. He defines a game as "an ongoing series of complementary ulterior transactions progressing to a well-defined, predictable outcome." Much of our transacting (Berne's way of describing our acting) consists of such games. Every game "is basically dishonest, and the outcome has a dramatic, as distinct from merely exciting, quality." Since we are dealing here with ulteriorly motivated behavior, and with "payoffs" for the actors, clearly much more than mere fun-and-games is at stake. Berne's popular reputation derives mainly from his insightful analysis and witty discussion of a variety of specific games—categorized as life games, marital games, sexual games, party games, underworld games, and even consulting room games. (An aftermath of this, as we know, was a whole slew of books with titles like *Games Alcoholics Play*, and *Games Psychiatrists Play*. Game designating became, indeed, an important new game.)

Basically, these games represent efforts by the individuals to achieve the most satisfactory payoff through their interaction. Each actor seeks to put himself or herself in the right or otherwise in a strong psychological position, while at the same time attempting to cast the partner-in-interaction into a wrong or weak one. To cite just one illustrative example: In the game "If It Weren't For You" the insecure woman marries a domineering man who will restrict her activities and thus keep her out of frightening situations. Then, however, "she takes advantage of the situation to complain about the restrictions," which leads her husband to feel uneasy, and may give her new power leverage over him. This also provides the basis for another game she can play with her woman friends, namely "If It Weren't For Him."

Though interaction games may prove to be individually or mutually destructive, or to promote undesirable types of interacting, they reflect (according to this view) the human being's natural attempt to maximize satisfactions. And their inevitability is ensured by the conditions of our society that provide little opportunity for real intimacy in our everyday contacts. They are, states Berne, "both necessary and desirable, and the only problem at issue is whether the games played by an individual offer the best yield for him." In a sense, "games" comes close to being Berne's term for culture. He asserts that games are passed on from generation to generation, that child rearing consists mainly of teaching about right and wrong games, and that people's associations tend to be organized around mutual game preferences.

Toward the end of *Games People Play*, Berne writes briefly about the desirability of personal autonomy—manifested or released (as we might have guessed) through awareness, spontaneity, and intimacy. On how we are to get there, especially given our proclivity for these games, he is not very clear. Though much of his analysis has been geared to highlighting the pathological qualities in specific games, he seems at the end to be largely reconciled to their perpetuation. All he can tell us is that "certain fortunate people" achieve awareness, intimacy, and spontaneity. The rest, who are unprepared for this, may be better off as they are. His rather despairing conclusion is: "This may mean that there is no hope for the human race, but there is hope for individual members of it."[18]

If this game-oriented view of social life avoids the optimistic excesses of much writing on awareness, it may hold the

danger of pushing us too hastily toward the other extreme—
of cynicism and ruthless self-advancement. In some ways, it
seems to be based on a realistic assessment of what's going on
in social interaction. There is a large body of literature on
interpersonal conflict and on "games theory" exploring the
patterns that emerge when people try to maximize their self-
interests. And psychiatrists have recognized that long-term
interpersonal relationships often are grounded in interlocking
and complementary neuroses or other pathological manifestations (in other words, games). Humorous depictions of how
satisfying success through interpersonal ploy can be (Berne
himself acknowledges the work of Stephen Potter on "gamesmanship" and "one-upmanship") often seem to strike home.
Influential sociological formulations, such as Erving Goffman's analysis of the "presentation of self" (in which we are
to a large extent seen as actors engaged in "the arts of impression management"),[19] similarly provide intellectual support for Berne's approach.

Ignoring interpersonal conflict will not cause it to go away.
In fact this is one of the difficulties with the more typical
self-awareness view that openness and honesty will make
everything all right. At the same time, realism does not necessarily require that we view all social behavior as exploitative
and prepare ourselves only to do battle accordingly. Both in
motivation and as regards even intended consequences (let
alone the unintended ones) human behavior is magnificently
variable. We are most assuredly not angels, yet neither are we
exclusively beasts. Belief that we are can become a self-fulfilling prophecy—much like the similarly "realistic" notion
that wars are inevitable. If our fear of being exploited (literally) gets the better of us, then our efforts to take over the
manipulating—along with those of the people whose fear is
of us—could themselves add up to the interpersonal warfare
of which we were afraid.

The relationship-advising message is compounded still further when the hard-headed assertiveness and gamesmanship

arguments are brought together (in one and the same presentation) with the optimistically instinct-trusting formulations more common to awareness writings. Since the former approach warns us about and even at times prepares us to compete in mutual exploitation, the two outlooks seem next to impossible to reconcile. Nonetheless, this highly confusing mixture can be found in some of the new self-improvement books. Consistency is not a strong point of the authors of such works. The greater the number of seductively "innovative" outlooks and techniques they can offer, the better.

Such a mixture begins to come across in the recent popularization of Berne's ideas presented by Thomas A. Harris in *I'm OK—You're OK*. Harris devotes a great deal of attention to the ego states or "life positions" (Parent–Adult–Child), aspects of which foul up people's lives and relationships. While he sees these as deeply built into the personality (and describes this through elaborate analogies to tape recordings, computers, and other technological apparatus), Harris remains pretty optimistic about overcoming their impact. "We cannot erase the recording," he writes," but we can choose to turn it off." The most desirable constellation of self- and other-concepts (namely, the "I'm OK—You're OK" of the title) he describes as being "a conscious and verbal decision." Three less healthy constellations (including the typical "You're OK—I'm not OK") are *based on feelings.*" "*The fourth is based on thought, faith, and the wager of action.* The first three have to do with *why*. The fourth has to do with *why not?*"

Transactions and games based on these "recordings" cause us a lot of emotional and interpersonal trouble. But apparently once you recognize and analyze them, the path to happiness and good relations presents itself. As people become able to strengthen the reality-oriented adult in themselves, and to accept the I'm OK—You're OK position, relationships of intimacy become possible. Harris's lyric description of such relationships runs as follows: "Giving and sharing are spon-

taneous expressions of joy, . . . Intimacy is a game-free relationship, since goals are not ulterior. . . . a situation where
the absence of fear makes possible the fullness of perception,
where beauty can be seen apart from utility, where possessiveness is made unnecessary by the reality of possession."[20] Exactly how this almost excruciatingly desirable state of affairs
is to be brought about, we are never really told. In true aware-
ness-movement fashion, Harris simply tells us that it can be
done. (And supports this claim with statistics showing 84
percent "success" with married couples in his group-treatment
program.)

The conversion of the games-theory orientation into an
explicit strategy to improve relating, and its combination with
self-help optimism, is advanced still further in several books
coauthored by group therapist George R. Bach. So far at least
two of these mass-marketed books (*The Intimate Enemy* and
Creative Aggression) have been built around Bach's idea of
"creative fighting," a notion that also has been picked up, in
one form or another, by many of the new do-it-yourself psychological-help books. A catchy thesis—couples who fight together will be right together! Bach comes on as a hard-headed
realist, asserting that ignorance is hardly ever bliss and that
bottled-up anger and hostility are lying just beneath the surface of most relationships. Claiming that the crisis of the
American family rests largely on our "inability to manage
personal conflicts," he asserts that (in addition to all those
divorces) "Millions of other couples continue to live together
physically and legally, yet emotionally apart."

There is a taboo on expressing anger in our society, and
partly for this reason we frequently exhibit "fight evasion
tendencies." (One often gets the impression in Bach's work
that continuous combat is the major criterion of mental
health.) Although Bach sees aggressive impulses as being more
natural than would some other "expressivist" writers, he is at
one with them in considering open expression of feelings the
path to intimacy. He wants to systematize aggression, to use it

as a tool (not just for catharsis, though that's part of his idea too—but also to heal the wounds in relationships). Yet at the same time, his writings are liberally sprinkled with references to preserving spontaneity. In the notion of "constructive fighting" Bach brings together the expressivist and better-communication themes of the new self-help movement. By fighting creatively, we will give free rein to our own feelings, and also get new and useful feedback about how the partner really feels.

According to Bach, we should fight "by appointment only," and (amazingly) it's often best to fight when other people are present—perhaps even the children. He does not support overtly physical combat, but does state we must face up to its pervasiveness. The important thing in nonviolent altercations is to fight constructively, which means openly and fairly—and for a purpose. Aimless fighting is out. "Couples who fight regularly and constructively need not carry gunny sacks full of grievances, and their psychiatric museums can be closed down." By studying "tens of thousands of intimate encounters," Bach and his associates have produced a "system" which they describe as being more in the way of a cooperative skill (like dancing) than a violent sport (such as boxing). "It is a tool, a way of life that paradoxically leads to greater harmony between intimates. . . . it can serve not only to enrich the lives of husbands, wives, and lovers; it could become the first step toward controlling the violent feelings that lead to assassinations and to aggressions between entire peoples."

The system for achieving this tall order is not really very complicated. Basically, it adds up to organizing and then analyzing your arguments and fights. (In this respect, again, it is more instrumental and thought-oriented than many self-awareness schemes.) Constructive fighting is open and honest. It means fighting fair. Also, being on the alert for unhealthy and counterproductive fight techniques—such as depersonalizing the partner and improperly exploiting advantages. This matter of comparative advantage lies at the heart of the system. It also may well be the system's undoing.

Bach acknowledges that "the only way to win intimate encounters is for both partners to win." Yet he sees no great difficulty in arranging things so as to ensure such an outcome. Thus he has "designed an entirely original fight-scoring system that determines neither 'losers' nor 'winners.' It gauges with considerable precision just how any fight affects the state of the union for a particular couple." Was the relationship's balance tipped in a constructive or destructive direction? According to Bach, we can systematically determine this by recording our battles on his "Fight Elements Profile" and "Fight Effects Profile" charts. He never explains why we should expect fighting partners to achieve consensus on the "scoring" and evaluation of their combat, or to accept a claim that neither contender has bettered the other. Apparently if Bach tells them there are no winners and losers, they will agree.

Fair fighting requires "an open encounter where both partners' 'weights' and weapons are equalized as much as possible." How can this be managed? Here, Bach relies heavily on mutual good will (presumably, the overriding desire to maintain the relationship). He states that Berne was excessively pessimistic. People want to overcome their game-playing tendencies. And, apparently, they want to fight fairly—if only they can be taught how to do so. Therefore, they will be prepared to learn about a partner's "belt line," and to honor it. Not to foul the partner, perhaps in effect even to give fighting handicaps. If this willingness to fight honorably and for mutual goals seem badly at odds with our supposedly seething anger and our realistic pursuit of our own interests, don't let it bother you. Bach says creative fighting is no universal panacea. All it can do is produce real intimacy, reduce riots, criminality, and warfare! "The more the values of realistic and aggressive intimacy pervade a culture, and the more people commit themselves to constructive verbal fighting, the more safely sated will be man's appalling appetite for lethal violence."[21]

In *Pairing: How to Achieve Genuine Intimacy*, Bach applies some of his ideas on human nature and interaction to the beginning, as well as the maintenance, of relationships. Here the call to take action is more direct and the optimism unbounded. "By the millions, men and women yearn for intimate love and cannot find it—not knowing how easily intimacy can be experienced, how effectively the emptiness can be filled." Once again, Bach has a system. It allows one to overcome the fears, angers, and false beliefs that prevent real intimacy. It has been taught to a great many men and women and "has proven almost invariably, often startlingly, effective."

Apart from being a peppy catchword, just what is pairing? Bach describes it as a new way of "making love begin." Actually, the book seems little more than a panegyric to the virtues of openness and assertiveness, along with criticism of some frequently encountered relating outlooks. There is a chapter explaining why computer dating is not likely to work well. Another warns about the self-defeating and unrealistic expectations of idealized romantic love. People must get over their fear of rejection. Here are some interpersonal exercises that may help us to do this. We must avoid relationships that involve "thinging." Instead, we should relate to the whole and unique person, in his or her own right. We should, at the start, be realistic about our relating partners. We should recognize their limitations, and explore with them the potential areas of conflict.

Where one seeks intimacy doesn't matter. Rather, it's how one goes about this that counts. Intimacy, it seems, is all around us—there for the taking—if we would but avail ourselves of the opportunities. The best way to do this is to develop our "valency" or "combining capacity" ("The key is the exposing of the genuine, here and now feelings to another"), and to "become more skilled as intimizers." We must try to read the nonverbal messages people send out. We must practice and learn(!) the "genuine" expression of interest in, and curiosity about, other people. Our efforts to satisfyingly relate must be imbued with "I-type" aggression (impacting—the demand for recognition as a total person) and not "H-type" (hostile) aggression. We must have accurate impressions of others, and convey effective impressions of ourselves.

Bach insists that such efforts need not amount to exploitation, which is "largely the result of thinging by one or both partners." By freely exchanging feelings, partners will develop a trust that reduces exploitation anxiety. Since elsewhere he takes a distinctly nonsexist position (for example, stating that sex-linked differences in temperament have been exaggerated and that male and female "fighting techniques" are pretty much interchangeable), one of his comments on exploitation through "thinging" is quite surprising: "We suggest that when a woman feels *continuously* thinged, it is because she things herself, causing others to treat her as a thing." Whatever the relating problems, Bach is able to come up with a pat solution. For example, he provides an eight-point checklist to determine your capacity to engage in "multiple pairing" (several love relationships simultaneously). He admits however (in neat formula fashion) that only if a person can respond positively on six of the eight items should they attempt this "ambitious and energy-demanding mode of behavior."[22]

An even more blatant invitation to engage in manipulative relating, is Julius Fast's *Body Language*. This book neatly illustrates the apparent irresistibility for American authors of the "how to" format. It starts off in a quite serious and detached manner, as a straightforward popularization of research findings and theories in the field of kinesics (nonverbal communication). Gradually it progresses, or degenerates (depending on your point of view) into an explicit guide for using "body language" to make sexual pickups and to create false impressions. Explaining to the reader about cross-cultural differences in the use of space, body position, or gesture is fine. So is elaborating the "wisdom of the body" theme to emphasize how nonverbal cues may increase our understanding of human behavior. But Fast's explicit advocacy of the use of these ideas to exploit potentially sexual situations hardly seems calculated to advance the cause of mutually rewarding relationships.

Thus a chapter on "The Silent Language of Love" describes with quite apparent approval how a successful "ladies' man" operates. Using throughout the language of predation, Fast takes us a very long way from "meaningful relationships," or even Bach's aggressive "impacting." He asks: "How does Mike single out his victim? What body language does an available girl at a party use to say, 'I'm available. I'm interested. I can be had.'? There must be a definite set of signals because Mike rarely makes a mistake." References to "the aggressor," "the complete arsenal of the woman on the warpath," and moving in on "the quarry's territory," permeate this bellicose scene. Subheadings that include "Choose Your Posture" and "Bedroom Eyes" are a dead giveaway to the book's encouragement of manipulative behavior.

In a last chapter on the "use and abuse" of body language, Fast notes the way in which political figures whose ideological constituency may be limited generate much wider appeal through a command of body language. For example, he ascribes to William Buckley (really a writer more than a politician) "an excellent command of the subtler nuances of kinesics. . . . The total effect is one of liveliness and animation, and adds sincerity to his statements." He cites various politicians who project this same "sincerity," and mentions others whose ideas may be good but for whom an ineffective use of gesture and expression has been an impediment. "The really good ones, good in the sense that they can project any emotion with their bodies, never had to bother about what they said. It was always the way they said it that mattered."

The problem, of course, is not whether this is an accurate description of events, but rather how we should evaluate such behavior. Naturally, Fast does not come right out and say it is

a good thing to go around consciously projecting "sincerity."
He does at the very least, however, seem to feel such behavior
is inevitable (that people will interpret nonverbal cues anyway, so we might as well make them good). And at times it's
hard to avoid the impression that he really admires this kind
of skill. Here's the way he concludes the book: "You've been
playing the game of body language unconsciously all of your
lifetime. Now start playing it consciously. Break a few rules
and see what happens. It will be surprising and sometimes a
bit frightening, adventurous, revealing and funny, but I promise you it won't be dull."[23]

Interpersonal Laissez-Faire

Current literature on relating displays, then, a variety of self-
awareness themes. It also exemplifies many of the movement's
internal contradictions and ironies. We find here assorted bits
and pieces of a far from unified and consistent outlook. In
any of the new relating manuals, we encounter a larger number of these disparate elements grouped together to form a
simplistic compendium of awareness-oriented relating lore. All
of which is offered to help the reader overcome his or her
relating inadequacies. One point, apparently, is never in
doubt. As the authors of *Intimate Feedback* put it, "we live
in a society where people are finding it increasingly difficult
to relate to one another and consequently to themselves."[24]

This very insistence may, of course, backfire. Does it help
more than it alarms? Telling other people that their relationships are no good (and that, in the last analysis, they themselves are responsible) is a risky business—quite apart from the
arrogance and condescension it may involve. Insisting that
people are out of touch, physically and figuratively, may
heighten their insecurities rather than lead them along the
path to feeling more secure. Likewise, a systematically engi-
neered "intimacy" may render real intimacy impossible.

None of this seems to bother the self-help disseminators

much. They are eager to provide all the help they can think of. *Intimate Feedback* illustrates the range of helpfulness. It has sections on body awareness and body relaxation, and numerous exercises for improving verbal and nonverbal communication. It discusses the importance of "learning to fight effectively," and provides techniques for practicing and enhancing decision-making. It urges partners to explore their use of time, to get to know each other better by exchanging and discussing "I believe" lists, lists of items on which each feels they disagree, and even "marriage obituaries." It discusses the importance of infusing sexual relations with a spirit of openness and honesty. It even has a handy rundown of possible new life styles and "alternatives to legal marriage."[25]

Above all the emphasis, as its title indicates, is on open and expressive communication. Relating advisors assume that partners don't really know each other, and that they don't know how to talk to each other. They also assume—in line with what we have seen is a central awareness notion—that open and honest communicating can solve most problems. All of these underlying premises are at least to some extent questionable. As indeed is the basic presupposition that individuals are creating their own unhappiness by not relating in the right ways. And when these relating specialists get down to the nitty-gritty of teaching us how to relate better, they fall into the same dilemma that previously confronted the authors of "enlightened" sex and marriage manuals. The more they tried to show us specific techniques for enjoying the wonders of sex, the more sex began to seem like work. We are almost at the point, today, where the same could be said of all "relating."

Taking seriously the constant admonition to relate better may lead people to accept uncritically the narrow interpersonal focus with which the self-awareness specialists would have us view our lives. The fuss about relating likewise reinforces a false belief that we can manage life by using content-free skills. But most ominously, the current approach to relating tends, as we have just seen, to shade off into implicit approval, if not open advocacy, of what can only be described as morally reprehensible behavior. To the extent it does that, it begins to defeat its own professed aims.

Basically, this is a matter of values. Most serious theorists of self-realization stress the primacy of humanistic values. Thus for Maslow the relationships of persons achieving that much-desired Being-cognition (and B-love) are unselfish, and "object-centered rather than ego-centered."[26] Yet the assertion of moral preferences and priorities is perpetually undermined by the value-free process emphasis of the awareness enhancers. This is particularly true in the popular personal-improvement books. For example, Jerry Greenwald, despite his expressed commitment to decency, and his recognition that nobody can be completely self-determining, ends up saying that in intimate relations "all shoulds are poison."[27]

What he means by this is that neither partner should be permitted to impose his or her values on the other. In similar fashion, he cites "blaming" as another feature of toxic, rather than nourishing, relating. The danger in such ideas is that a repudiation of arbitrary value-imposing, may end up looking remarkably like a repudiation of all values. Only in some presumed moral vacuum could the more blatantly manipulative and impression-management types of "aware" behavior be acceptable. Many writers on self-awareness seem to recognize this problem. They attempt to deal with it by engaging in some rather fancy distinction-drawing. Hence, we hear that there is a world of difference between self-assertiveness and naked aggression; that we should distinguish between "negative power" (ability to control force, kill, etc.) and "positive power" (influencing others and getting one's needs met in a loving way, and without any necessity of pressure). According to Philip Slater, "The need for negative power is expressive of the lack of positive power. The less positive power one has, the more negative power one needs."[28]

Such disclaimers are not fully persuasive. What one person

may take to be positive power or healthy assertiveness, another may see as blatantly aggressive exploitation. Where does all this leave the bewildered reader, or client of a "growth" program? Most likely, more at sea than ever. First, he or she is told that human beings are warm, honest, and generous—if only they're given the chance. Then comes the contradictory message that you can count on nobody to look out for you but yourself, that we are surrounded by self-interested schemers, and that we had better fight fire with fire.

What seems ultimately to emerge out of this very mixed message is an ethic of self-preservation. Within the awareness movement, optimists and cynics agree in placing final responsibility on the lone individual. Whether you can satisfy your real needs by simply being, or whether instead you'll need to employ rational machinations, either way it is up to you. Hence we arrive at a picture of relationships governed by "free competition"—a kind of interpersonal laissez-faire. A "natural" adversary system, in which—just as was assumed in the economic theory of laissez-faire—self-interested and open efforts by both sides should produce justice and keep the system working smoothly. Whether they realize it or not, advocates of self-awareness apparently believe that once we are aware and self-reliant, an invisible hand will guide our relationships along these desirable paths.

Like their counterparts in economic theory, the spokesmen for awareness give little recognition to inequalities in bargaining power. The interpersonal marketplace could conceivably work if all competitors were equal in all pertinent ways. Clearly they are not. Just as "freedom of contract" was a most misleading term, so therefore is "freedom of relating." People, in fact, are not equally free in relating—any more than in anything else. Nor can many of these inequalities be attributed to either their innate or even culturally imposed deficiencies. Resources and bargaining power reflect the sociocultural context of relationships, as do the substantively patterned ways in which people relate. This fact alone highlights the gross simplification of most awareness ideas about relating. It also poses issues of crucial importance to the women's movement, to which we turn next.

V / Women and Awareness

The Sexual Politics of Awareness

Sexism, blatant or subtle, pervades contemporary American society. As the inadvertently sexist wording of the SDS "Port Huron" statement quoted earlier shows, even progressive and humanistically oriented movements are not immune from this sociocultural virus. (We know, in fact, that many women became disillusioned with the New Left precisely because it seemed organized as a male autocracy.) The movement to enhance self-awareness is no exception. It has had, and should continue to have, a significant role to play in igniting women's consciousness. But if followed in the wrong directions, it could hinder rather than support major advances for women.

The popular awareness message may be pitched particularly to a female audience. Because of their earlier exclusion from other realms, women (both stereotypically and actually) have dominated the field of emotional expression and preoccupation with interpersonal relations. It was this stereotyped domination that bred all those articles on "Holding Your Husband Without Jealousy." It was women's "social–emotional" concerns and problems that flooded the syndicated personal advice columns. Although I have not made a systematic content analysis of the relevant publications, I very much doubt that this pattern has changed a great deal.

Neither the inclusion of new types of materials in women's magazines (career-oriented articles, etc.), nor the advent of more political journals aimed at women, nor even the glimmerings of men's liberation, has really altered the tendency to locate the "feelings-oriented" readership primarily among women. Recent interest in self-awareness ideas and techniques fits into, rather than changes, this model. Thus writer Stephanie Harrington recently designated the very "with it" magazine *Cosmopolitan* as "the psychosexual self-help magazine." Citing editor Helen Gurley Brown's attempt to provide a dual emphasis on work and sex, she quotes Brown as saying that "sex pieces, get-man pieces are stronger, more frequent. . . . because I'm more caught up in the life of the emotions. . . . I *know intellectually* that jobs are as important. But they're not as good for *Cosmo* in terms of sales."[1]

A newsstand glance at women's magazines today shows that they are chock-full of new-awareness articles. Readers of the mass-appeal women's journals are gobbling up the latest word on body relaxation, nonverbal communications, and relating —along with the perennial tips on dieting, makeup, and fashion. So the old, not so carefully hidden, message is perpetuated. There is something wrong with women. They aren't dealing with other people correctly, anymore than they're taking care of themselves correctly. They had better, in short, shape up.

Perhaps it is not surprising that most of the awareness gurus are men. In large measure the movement perpetuates the well-

entrenched tendency for men to tell women what's wrong
with them, and then offer to do something about it. Of course,
the new gurus would deny this. They would insist they see all
humans simply as humans. That their message is aimed at,
and applies equally to, both men and women. However, as
some women are beginning to realize, their sex's constant
recourse to men in these advice relationships may be unfortunate—if not downright unhealthy. In the awareness movement,
the situation may not be all that different from the psy-
chotherapeutic one Phyllis Chesler criticizes in *Women and
Madness*. As she suggests, therapy (like marriage) typically
places the woman in a relationship of dependency with a
stronger male authority figure. "She wants from a psychother-
apist what she wants—and often cannot get—from a husband:
attention, understanding, merciful relief, a *personal solution*
—in the arms of the right husband, on the couch of the right
therapist."[2]

There is a sprinkling of women among the awareness promoters, but at most this represents a kind of tokenism. In
theory and practice alike, the movement has been dominated
by men. Even when they have had the best of intentions,
many of their efforts may indirectly have been weakening
women's position. Major aspects of the self-awareness outlook
remain ambiguous from the standpoint of women's liberation.
Themes that at first glance seem truly liberating turn out, on
closer analysis, to fall far short of the mark. Antipathy to form
and content is largely to blame. With little attention to issues
of substance, the likelihood of substantive gains for women is
meager indeed.

We see this, for example, in the way the movement treats
roles and role-playing. When we impute to the individual
power over and responsibility for the roles he or she plays, we
lose sight of the institutionalized context of patterns that
guide and constrain people. As we have already seen, there is
a great deal of talk in awareness circles about the unnatural
limitations placed on us by roles. Roles are the enemy, but

their substance and sources of support are slighted. If we ignore them, they will go away. To be sure, the utopian counter-culture theorists do not take this view. Nor do advocates of equality in marriage—although usually they believe that the partners revising their personal commitment will suffice to produce the necessary change. Yet, with those possible exceptions, the awareness literature strikingly and consistently fails to mention the substance of sex-role differentiation in our society.

One would hardly gather that women need liberation from anything but themselves. That our dominant child-rearing patterns, the content of the mass media, the underlying expectations and organization of our educational and occupational systems, or the composition of our legal codes have anything whatever to do with women's failure to achieve their "human potential." Clearly, most of the awareness-enhancers would (if asked) condemn the current social restrictions on and cultural expectations for women. But unasked, they remain silent on such matters. By acting as though "all that" goes without saying, they make sure it isn't said. Hence, their commendable aversion to restrictive roles ends up providing indirect support for the very conditions they mean (but fail explicitly) to condemn.

They can reduce almost any of the major women's issues to personal or interpersonal terms. Take the matter of housework. All too often, in this new literature, women are urged to give themselves over to the sensual satisfactions of cooking or cleaning. Obviously, this follows from the idea that what you do is not nearly as important as how you go about it, how you feel about it. There is a world of difference between this approach and that developed in the women's movement. As two able chroniclers of that movement, Judith Hole and Ellen Levine, have noted, "The use of the phrase 'politics of housework' is an indication of the nature of feminist analysis: the individual role definition applied to a woman serves a *social-political* function. A necessary job in society has been delegated to a group of people and rationalized on the basis of inherent personality (biologically-derived) traits. . . ."[3]

British feminist Sheila Rowbotham develops this point still further. Discussing the situation of women who earn their living by doing cleaning (an option which, as she notes, rarely represents the woman's own free choice), she goes on to recognize that other aspects of female participation in the labor market are similarly affected by our perception of women as homemakers. Something of this sort occurs among secretaries—who are there in the office to enhance its appearance and protect its smooth-runningness, to reassure the men and run errands for them even more than to get the actual work done. As Rowbotham provocatively suggests, "the notion of women's work as an extension of woman's role in the family serves to conceal that much of this work is hard and dirty; it also enables employers to retain paternalistic forms of control over women workers and extract more labour power from them which does not even find reflection in the wage packet."[4]

The complex social issue of abortion can likewise be reduced to its narrower personal and interpersonal dimensions. In her intriguing sexual memoir and analysis of women's situation, *Combat in the Erogenous Zone*, Ingrid Bengis expresses concern when she encounters an eighteen-year-old who is about to have an abortion. "Of course she shouldn't have a baby. Of course abortions make sense. But even if they do make sense, something is wrong with a world in which girls have abortions, rushed through nicely and efficiently. Motherhood cannot be taken all that lightly. . . . Which was not to say that I thought the abortion law should be repealed, or that I thought Janet was wrong to get an abortion, or that eighteen-year-old girls should be abstinent." Bengis tries to pull together this confusing set of reactions by asserting that abortions exist in a context, a context only secondarily medical and legal. "Its primary context remained, as it always had, in the realm of the human and the personal. Its primary context had to do with the quality of the relationships between men and women."[5]

Humane feelings—to an extent. But defining the problem's "primary context" in this narrow way requires setting aside much of the social reality of abortion-seeking situations. If we could attain perfection in our relationships, then presumably we could do without distasteful means of correcting the damage we do to each other. But such perfection is going to be a long time coming. While we are seeking it, we would do well to think also about making the best of less than perfect situations. If women are going to terminate unwanted pregnancies anyway, how can we condemn their doing so "nicely and efficiently"? Are we really prepared to prefer unsavory and unsafe illegal abortions? Bengis, of course, does not go so far as to say we should. Can we condone the gross social-class disparities in availability of relatively safe abortions that pertain under conditions of illegality? And can these facts be assessed in abstraction from a broader context of sexual and economic exploitation within which much of our relating occurs in the first place? No doubt Bengis is aware of some of these difficulties. Yet she persists in wanting to personalize the problem as much as possible. Perhaps it's for this reason that we can never really tell where she stands.

Characteristic awareness emphases on emotional expressiveness and sheer physicality also produce uncertain consequences for the women's movement. A general freeing up of the emotions among both sexes should (theoretically) help to undermine rigid and stereotyped notions about the behavior that's appropriate for each. However, in our society it seems to be men in particular who are deficient in this regard. Women, in a sense, already are too expressive. Their "innate" emotionalism and expressiveness lie at the core of the very stereotypes they now wish to overturn. So the emphasis on feelings could backfire, locking women even more completely into the circumscribed pattern from which they seek escape.

In deferring to men, women undoubtedly did bottle up

certain emotions that might better have been openly expressed. Hence the self-awareness call to "healthy anger" has great appeal. The cathartic value of such anger is clear. But this anger needs to be channeled beyond individual targets if it is to have more than just cathartic effect. Assertiveness training is especially useful on this score. It emphasizes goal-seeking and focuses emotional energy in positive directions. As we've seen, however, a specter of renewed manipulativism beclouds this asserting scheme. Women may begin to act in the (supposedly despised) ways men had previously used to subjugate them. To take what they can get, and the devil may care. To "use" men for their own purposes. To treat men as objects, sexual or otherwise.

A positive side of this is the repudiation of "double standards." A more negative aspect is that all standards may go out the window in the process. While women may thus help to defeat the stereotyped image of themselves as timid and dependent (an image they themselves often accepted), the satisfactions of taking over exploitative roles are not likely to last. Super-aggressive women are no nicer or happier than super-aggressive men. Above all, to become preoccupied with "scoring" may (perhaps as much as a preoccupation with being "taken") engulf women in the personalizing of life problems that has been impeding their collective advancement all along.

For women to become "man-hating" probably is, at this stage of the game, better than for them to be self-hating. But it would be depressing if a permanent residue of new or increased hatred turned out to be a legacy of the movement to enhance self-awareness and human potential. Of course, we are told the basis for hatred has been there all the time. The thing now is to face up to it. The danger, however, lies in women dissipating their emotional energies in a round of new interpersonal games—even if they now emerge more often as "winners" than as "losers." In the long run (and in the broader context of social advancement), such apparent winners may turn out to be real losers.

Man-hating, then, can be another interiorizing trap. Ingrid Bengis, who poignantly describes her efforts to avoid it, finds herself (because men continuously treat her as an object) overwhelmed by this response. She describes it as a defense, a refusal, and also an affirmation. "It is a defense against fear, against pain. It is a refusal to suppress the evidence of one's experience. It is an affirmation of the cathartic effects of justifiable anger." Yet in it too she sees the possibility for renewal. "For if I say today, 'I hate you,' it is in order that tomorrow it might perhaps be easier to say, 'I love you.' "[6] Does that sound suspiciously like the old open expressiveness, pain–joy, unity of "polarities" formula? If so, it's probably not surprising, for it reflects the closed circle of preoccupation with feelings and "relating" to which awareness thinking so often leads.

Feminists note that charges of "man-hating" often are used as a red herring, a catchy way of discrediting the women's movement. This tends to exaggerate its prevalence, and at the same time to distort the political meaning of defining men as the enemy. Judith Hole and Ellen Levine point out that, "Many radical feminists make a distinction between hate, which can be a paralyzing emotion, and anger. They argue that the recognition of oppression does indeed provoke anger and only by acknowledging this anger will women mobilize their energies to bring about change. Thus, the recognition of men as the 'class' enemy is in their analysis not only ideologically correct but tactically necessary."[7] The idea of mobilization for change is central here, as a corrective to the tendency toward objectless emotional expression. Women who uncritically absorb the self-awareness message can concentrate neither on long-term goals nor on the institutional framework of their exploitation. It is not just this man, or that man, but men in general who are the oppressors. And, above all, it is through man-made and man-advantaging social institutions, that men exert power and control over women. On this cardinal point, the awareness movement and the women's movement often seem to point in opposite directions.

Body consciousness similarly carries an ambiguous message for women. Awareness-enhancers and feminists are at one in saying we must place a positive value on the human body and on sensual pleasure. They agree that the restricted sense of joy we have been experiencing stems in part from undervaluing or disvaluing the body. As we saw earlier, emphasizing biophysiology contributes heavily to a narrow individualizing focus. Beyond that, however, is an even bigger problem for the women's movement. Body affirmation, in general, is a good thing. But just what kind of body affirmation should women want to encourage? On that issue, neither awareness enthusiasts nor feminists consistently provide sound guidance.

Women's bodies are as good as men's. Women as well as men should be free to enjoy sex. Women's bodies are nobody else's property. Insofar as possible women themselves should have control over their bodies. They are the ones who should decide what happens to, and in, their bodies. By now, these should be points of fairly general agreement—though admittedly this abstract consensus still bogs down badly when we try to implement these principles. At the very least, adopting a self-awareness viewpoint in no way runs counter to these important themes of the women's movement. But feminism involves much more than body consciousness. Body acceptance may be essential to changing women's situation. Body preoccupation is another story altogether.

Body preoccupation, after all, lies at the heart of treating women as sex objects. A version of it (which Naomi Weisstein nicely terms "the fundamentalist myth of sex-organ causality")[8] also underlies those psychological theories that have encouraged a narrow definition of women's natural behavior. There is, to be sure, a lively dispute about the precise extent to which Freudianism should be held accountable for all aspects of the "anatomy is destiny" argument.[9] Nonetheless, there is little doubt that in general the work of Freud and most of his followers—stressing "instinctual" drives and similar biologisms—helped convince people (women included) that females were "naturally" passive, nurturant, and emotional. As Vivian Gornick and Barbara Moran have commented, "Freudianism, though it promised freedom and seemed to challenge Puritanism, had been subverted to a privatism that served the status quo only too well."[10]

How do the new self-awareness body-emphasizers fit into this picture? It's really hard to be sure. They have no obvious intention of promoting sexism, or of hampering the women's movement. They insist they are opposed to social adjustment as a criterion of well-being. But it is difficult sometimes to distinguish between sexist and nonsexist body consciousness. The extremely popular exercise regimes associated with yoga and similar approaches presumably have no sexist connotations. They can be practiced by men as well as women—though I suspect that if statistics were available we would find that women clients predominate in these programs. Yet the emphasis on graceful movements and on shaping up, as well as the apparent shading-off of these programs into straightforward exercise-weight control ones, are ominous signs. One could, of course, insist that sexism is in the eye of the beholder. That these patently healthful activities ought not be condemned for their potential misuses. Nonetheless, it is striking that in these regimes women end up doing essentially what they have done before: trying to conform to the movie-star image of what will be pleasing to men, indirectly upholding the idea that how women look and feel is more important than what they do.

Self-awareness specialists such as Alexander Lowen may compound the message still further when they emphasize the release of orgasmic capacity as part of "reclaiming the body." He provides an ecstatic description of vaginal orgasm through intercourse, in which "the whole body becomes one big heart."[11] How one is to square this with feminist analyses insisting there is no such thing as "vaginal orgasm"—only orgasm generally, obtained by whatever means—is not clear.[12] But if some awareness urgers may deny women absolute in-

dependence in sexuality, others develop an even more extreme
position, in the opposite direction. Thus, certain assertiveness
advisors are now very big on having sex by yourself.

According to a recent account, there has been "considerable
underground proselytizing for masturbation in the women's
movement." Women are sponsoring masturbation workshops
and parties, giving each other "masturbatory homework assignments," and watching vibrator demonstrations. One self-
stimulation entrepreneur has even set up a "mail-order
sexuality boutique for women." An authoritative book on self-
stimulation by a West Coast sex therapist bears the apt title,
For Yourself.[13] It seems doubtful that this is what the wom-
en's movement should be about. Yet it may be where a
certain type of self-awareness leads: replacing sexual cold
war with sexual isolationism, turning male objectification of
women around the other way—as in the new male "nudie"
magazines for women. Women are beginning to "play around"
sexually, a pattern that ultimately should be no more satisfying to them than the compulsive conquest style has been for
men.[14]

Whether women are told they will achieve sexual joy via
dependence or via self-assertion, the result is pretty much the
same. Either way, the message is that their lives should revolve
around their bodies. That self-fulfillment is, essentially, sexual
fulfillment. The problem with all this is expressed nicely by
Phyllis Chesler, discussing Wilhelm Reich's ideas on sex. She
writes: "In a patriarchal culture it is destructively romantic to
talk too much about female 'surrender' in heterosexual intercourse and, for that matter, to talk too much about the importance of female sexual happiness, without talking about the
importance of female *power*. The use of sex, like drugs, can
become a compulsive pacification-opiate, especially to those
without the power to define themselves."[15]

Body preoccupation, in short, can seriously defuse the political momentum of the women's movement. When channeled into specific constructive directions—as it has been in

the trend to reevaluate the quality of medical advice and
health care women have been receiving—body consciousness
fits in well with other efforts to further women's goals.[16]
When simply let loose, and pushed to extremes, body preoccupation displaces more significant concerns and under-
mines collective action. Women's energies are drained by a
renewed sexual combat with men, or a persisting sexual competition with other women. As Sheila Rowbotham properly
states, "In the absence of a political movement we become
accomplices. . . . In isolation the individual woman who
passes over into activity is bound to define herself at the expense of other women."[17]

Raising Which Consciousness?

A narrowly based version of self-awareness could, then, have
boomeranging effects. Woman's subordinate position in our
society has, after all, rested in part on her willingness always
to turn inward. To accept a limited, and hence limiting, conception of herself and her place in the social order. To be
preoccupied with her body, her feelings, her relationships. To
use interpersonal relations as a primary avenue to self-esteem.
To interiorize or privatize numerous kinds of life problems,
and to believe that the ultimate "solutions" are individual
ones. As Phyllis Chesler emphasizes, women have been encouraged to talk (endlessly, about "their" personal problems),
rather than to act. Now, even more than before, under the
aegis of the new awareness advisors, they are being urged also
to emote, to respond to their own feelings.

Such interiorizing is a large part of the problem, not the
solution. Women already suffer because of the widely accepted notion of their essential *innerness*. In this regard, the
supposed experts on personality and behavior are themselves
partly to blame. Thus asserts Naomi Weisstein (herself a
psychologist, but also a feminist), "Psychologists must realize

that it is they who are limiting discovery of human potential
. . . when they assume that people move in a context-free
ether, with only their innate dispositions and their individual
traits determining what they will do. Until psychologists . . .
begin looking at the social contexts within which people
move, psychology will have nothing of substance to offer in
this task of discovery."[18] The new guidance specialists do not
seem likely to adopt the broader viewpoint.

For these reasons, "raising women's consciousness" is a
highly complicated process. Consciousness of what? Their
humanity, their unique individuality, their femaleness, or
their sisterhood? And what should they see as having held
back the desired consciousness—themselves, other women,
men, or society? The difficulty in answering such questions is,
needless to say, heightened for those women who have been
multiply disadvantaged under our present system—such as
working-class women, black (brown or red) women, and
lesbian women. Women's liberation inevitably involves coming to terms with these and other similarly compounded
situations. Complex problems usually call for complex solutions. Each of the elements of women's consciousness I just
mentioned can be valid and useful. It is the skewing of perspective (in the direction of a misplaced individualizing) that
is dangerous. As we've seen, current promoters of self-awareness gloss over all these complexities. We can be happy and
fulfilled, they keep telling us, if we become aware of our
human feelings and our unique individuality, if we recognize
that our own lack of responsibility is hampering this consciousness. Indeed, as I've already suggested, their prescription often comes close to being nothing more than a
consciousness of consciousness itself.

Even if viewed in the best possible light, this course of
action (really, inaction) could not get women very far. Yet it
may hold a strong seductive appeal for them. To some extent
this is due precisely to the fact that it reinforces and further
legitimates the outlooks to which they're already accustomed.

Chesler points out that American middle-class women feel at home in psychiatric careers. The same could be said of careers in self-awareness. Women have long been socialized to accept this kind of passive self-absorption. Then too, there must be a special temptation to accept the "emotional superiority of women" argument that sometimes creeps into thinking of this sort. If women are naturally passive, supporting, and loving, perhaps there's really no need for a women's movement at all. Thus we find George Gilder arguing that what is needed instead, for "the very achievement of human civilization," is the "submission of male to female nature. The men have to leave their battles and hunts and whorings and commit their energies to the building and supporting of homes and the celebration of women."[19] Clearly, women achieve a certain kind of gain from this "celebration"—albeit a deceptive one. Particularly for the comfortable middle-class traditionalist, it isn't so easy to come down from the pedestal.

Woman's awareness is strongly influenced by the fact that her social and economic exploitation seems inextricably tied up with "internal" aspects of her consciousness. Sheila Rowbotham aptly refers to the rule of men over women as "a rather gentle tyranny." She points out that this often takes the form of an "ecstatic subjugation," that it is "very different from the relationship between worker and capitalist."[20] Ambivalence toward the "oppressor," and a heavy focus on emotional consciousness seem natural to this situation. Even the most militant of the women's movement theorists are hard put to define woman's quest solely in sociopolitical or economic terms.

Thus Shulamith Firestone, a radical feminist whose concept of women's freedom extends to advocacy of "artificial reproduction," warns against letting feminist priorities be "tailored to fit into a preexistent (male-created) political framework." In her view, "Politico women are unable to evolve an authentic politics because they have never truly confronted their oppression *as women* in a gut way."[21] Kate

Millett, whose *Sexual Politics* was a major contribution to the developing women's movement, insists that "the arena of sexual revolution is within human consciousness even more preeminently than it is within human institutions."[22] And Juliet Mitchell, the British Marxist-oriented feminist, comments that it has been a growing consciousness of women's "mental and emotional debasement" that has permitted them to recognize their economic oppression. From this standpoint, she argues, the predominantly middle-class composition of the organized women's movement is to be expected, for "poverty alone cannot protest for itself." At any rate, the oppression of women is as much cultural as economic. "Women are an oppressed half of the population."[23]

We might be tempted to say that when even such activists stress woman's personal and emotional situation, this fact itself reflects the "traditional" female obsession with such matters. Yet a good deal more seems to be at stake. Woman's situation is unique. It cuts across many of the usual social, political, and economic categories. And the very nature of her exploitation combines in special ways elements of personal identity and institutional structure. This is what feminists mean when they use the term "sex class." It is what the New York Radical Feminists tried to highlight in an influential 1969 manifesto: "The political oppression of women has its own class dynamic; and that dynamic must be understood in terms previously called 'non-political'—namely the politics of the ego."[24]

For most organized feminists, then, social change that has real meaning for women requires eliminating sexism. And to do this we need somehow to politicize the "personal" or personalize the political. We need to root out a special psychology of oppression that both motivates males and permeates the social system. The combination of structurally and personally oppressive elements is evident in numerous aspects of a woman's daily experience. Can she get a decent job, and how well can she expect to do there? (On the more "personal" level—How do the men she knows feel about women's work? How do the women she knows, and she herself, feel about it?) How free is she socially to shape her sexual life in her own way? (And what attitudes towards women's sexuality does she directly encounter in her everyday contacts with people and in her own intimate relationships?) If she has children, what kinds of child-rearing assistance (financial, practical, etc.) does she have access to? (What attitudes do those around her take toward woman's child-rearing role?)

So it goes, through virtually all of her life situations. No doubt the direct experiencing of sexism means much more to the average woman than an abstract knowledge of institutionalized patterns and restrictions. Hence the exhortation to women to acknowledge and build on their own "gut" responses. However, as Juliet Mitchell points out, this "politics of experience," liberating as it may be, has distinct limitations. It can easily have the effect of dampening more profound rebellion. To focus on feelings "ignores its really oppressive side within our society. Emotions cannot be 'free' or 'true' in isolation: they are dependent today on a social base that imprisons and determines them."[25]

Women's consciousness-raising groups aim to develop and put to use a dual personal–institutional focus on sexist oppression. These groups often reflect human-potential ideas, to which many of the members had been exposed earlier. The overall approach at first glance seems highly reminiscent of encounter grouping. Small groups of women meeting informally and "rapping together," sharing their feelings, breaking down feelings of isolation and developing trust, expressing their anger and receiving support, enhancing self-understanding and empathy, building bonds of affection through a common group experience with people who may previously have been perfect strangers.

There is, however, a crucial difference. CR groups have a specific substantive focus. Members are not simply expressing

any and all feelings and experiences—for the sake of such
expression. Rather, they are zeroing in on their feelings and
experiences *as women.* We see this in the characteristic topics
of CR "raps." What attitudes toward girls were reflected in
members' early childhood experiences? What were their first
sexual experiences like? How have their situations as women
been affected by the educational system and in the occupational realm? What attitudes toward marriage were they
brought up with? How do they feel about pregnancy and
motherhood? How has the cultural emphasis on women being
"beautiful" affected their lives? What are their attitudes toward other women, and toward men? How have they been
treated by male gynecologists? Have they, or any of their
friends, ever been raped? How do they feel about abortion?
Or homosexuality? Do they see religion as having helped
them or hurt them, as women? What are their feelings about
aging? Have they been in psychotherapy, and how did this
experience affect (or how was it affected by) their womanhood? How do they feel about other races, and are there
similarities between racism and sexism?[26]

Most of these groups have been mainly middle-class in composition, and this is reflected in the selection of topics. Invariably, too, the starting point (as we can see here) is direct
personal experience and gut reactions. When CR groups
began springing up in the early 1960s, sharp factionalism arose
within some women's organizations over just this issue. Politically oriented women argued that all the talk about feelings
was meaningless. Others insisted that conventional political
ideas and actions did not do justice to the special needs of
feminism. Feelings, they claimed, could be made political:
"Our feelings will lead us to ideas and then to actions. Our
feelings will lead us to our theory, our theory to our action,
our feelings about that action to new theory and then to new
action."[27]

Similar differences in orientation continue today, and undoubtedly there is a very wide variety of types of women's

groups. How much a specific group's discussion will take on a psychological emphasis, and how much a political one, will depend on its particular makeup. But usually the focus on womanhood will lead the group beyond the self-enclosed and apolitical expressivism that encounter sessions frequently promote. As Claudia Dreifus comments, in her excellent personal account and analysis of CR groups, "Consciousness raising is one of the most political acts in which women can engage. In CR, women learn what economics, politics, and sociology mean on the most direct level: as they affect their lives."[28]

This kind of awareness—along with the increased self-confidence and sense of sisterhood the group process generates—often may lead to direct political actions. Whether the members move in this overtly activist direction or not, however, the consciousness that has been raised is almost always political in the broadest sense of the term. Women find that what they thought were personal problems are in fact common, shared problems—problems that are institutionalized, that are grounded in a sociocultural framework, oppression that is collective, and not individual. "Consciousness raising," notes Dreifus, "is many things, but one thing it is *not* is psychotherapy, or any other kind of therapy. Therapeutic processes have been employed mostly to encourage participants to adjust to the social order. CR seeks to invite rebellion."[29]

Indeed, perhaps the major contribution of consciousness raising has been to show women that many of the problems they previously would have viewed as personal symptoms are really social symptoms: to illuminate insufficiently recognized processes of sex-role stereotyping, to expose the systematic restrictions that uphold narrowly prescribed social roles for women, to reveal the patterned and socially supported inequalities that underlie male dominance. In short, to develop an awareness that "Sexism, like any other cultural characteristic, lives through institutions—those that blindly perpetuate it and those that depend upon it for their very life."[30]

There is always the danger of CR backsliding into something more akin to group therapy. Commenting on the influence of encounter-group ideas, Juliet Mitchell warns of "the fate of the whirlpool"—in which the members' self-concerns become all-enveloping.[31] Particularly in the United States, where the tradition of radical political activity is so poorly developed, women's groups can easily slip into this kind of dead-end format. Here, commitment to the cause of women can make the vital difference. Commercialization of CR, by uncommitted outsiders, could be the kiss of death. Dreifus refers to "unscrupulous psychotherapists" who are jumping onto the consciousness-raising bandwagon. Worse yet, she notes, and reports that "the guys who made a killing on encounter groups" are "now considering setting up consciousness-raising businesses. Instead of conducting screaming matches for a fee, they would now hire themselves out to organize sisterhood!"[32]

Sexism and Women's Potential

If such pitfalls are avoided, consciousness-raising can become a significant mechanism for broadening as well as intensifying awareness. Then, the basic lesson learned is this: institutionalized sexism is the major barrier to the achievement of women's potential. Such a conclusion rests, of course, on a rather different conception of potential than the amorphous one that pervades the self-awareness movement. To be sure, sexism prevents women from leading fully creative, productive, and joyous lives. But this state of affairs reflects a great many specific restrictions placed on women in diverse areas of activity and a variety of misplaced emphases in our cultural priorities and dominant values. It is not simply a consequence of (though it may also involve) people's failure to be open, honest, and aware. It is built into our system, and should not be attributed to alleged deficiencies of women themselves.

Already, the accumulated documentation of sexism and its
institutional groundings is overwhelming.[33] Systematic discrimination against women, and blatantly sexist (anti-woman)
values, are so pervasive in our society that it is difficult to
know where to start in attempting even a highly sketchy summary. Women have been unfairly denied equal access to and
advancement in educational programs, and in most occupational realms. They have been paid less than men for the
same work. Many of our laws (and the administration of
justice) in diverse substantive areas—such as property, bank-
ing, domestic relations, housing, and criminal law—are slanted
against women. Prostitutes are jailed; their male clients generally are not. Administrative and legal rulings under welfare
programs often improperly curtail women's rights. The divorced woman is stigmatized; the divorced man is not.
Women who have been raped are treated as wrongdoers,
rather than as victims. Prior to recent court rulings, male-
dominated legislatures were free to greatly restrict women's
legal right to terminate unwanted pregnancies. Our entire
system of advertising has been heavily geared to the exploitation of women as sex objects. The mass media, in addition to
incorporating this practice, widely disseminate various false
stereotypes of women. Mistaken notions about the "natural"
behavior of each sex permeate our child-rearing practices, and
the formal education of our children.

We are beginning to see change in most of these areas. But
it is not being brought about because of new techniques for
self-awareness. Change is resulting from focused and collective efforts to achieve specific goals. This means organization
and hard work, systematic collection of statistics, comparative analyses and large-scale research, putting pressure on
political candidates and lobbying in legislatures, bringing test
cases to challenge discrimination, disseminating accurate information and exposing ignorance and bias, fighting prejudice
and overcoming the vested interests that often buttress inequality. Being in touch with one's feelings and natural sur-

roundings may help, but it can never be a substitute for such efforts.

Though recent advances for women may at first seem impressive, actually they have only begun to scratch the surface. New York City Human Rights Commissioner Eleanor Holmes Norton has recently stated: "Despite the beginnings of gains on the employment and other fronts as a result of the pressures brought by the women's movement and, indeed, despite the continuing socioeconomic changes which have gradually shifted male–female roles for much of the last century, the nation is still in the primitive stage when it comes to offering women equal opportunity." She goes on to note that the average working woman works of economic necessity (not in order to have a career). Usually she is underpaid. And our society "has failed miserably to provide what most other industrialized countries have taken for granted for decades: namely, widely available, publicly sponsored or publicly subsidized child care." This is but a small part of the persisting sex inequality in the area of employment alone. Norton cites a range of related phenomena: discrimination in hiring and advancement, inequality in admission to graduate, professional, and technical schools; the "stamp of 'masculinity' on jobs ranging from banker to television repairman—jobs which require no 'masculine' trait for performance"; men's unchanging attitudes towards women's work; inadequate awareness by women themselves of the full dimensions of their situation.[34]

Specific targets for social change to advance women's interests are many. New York City's Commission on Human Rights grouped its more than one hundred recommendations relating to women's role under the following broad categories —Employment (including proposals for change in business and industry, professions, government, state labor law, pregnancy and fringe benefits); Household Workers; Taxation; Social Services (child care, income maintenance for welfare mothers, family planning); Housing and Credit Practices; Education (fourteen recommendations in this field alone);

Law (equal rights protection, family law, penal law, jury duty); and Politics.[35] Hole and Levine's survey of the women's movement notes that recent feminist activity has been concentrated in six major areas: Media, Abortion, Child Care, Education, Professions, and the Church.[36] Juliet Mitchell, an important theoretical interpreter of women's liberation, emphasizes the complex interconnections between spheres of oppression. She points to four interrelated domains requiring transformation: Production, Reproduction, Sexuality, and Socialization.[37]

We must recognize, then, that women are enmeshed in a generalized system of domination. Their subordination is a central feature of our entire way of life. Its manifestations appear in quite diverse social institutions and behavior patterns. They have economic and political ramifications, as well as being tied together through interlocking features of our social structure. They reflect a deep-seated cultural devaluing of women. Claims about women's allegedly "special" qualities (warmth, intuition, etc.) mask the denigration of their intelligence and overall competence. This is the true stifling of their potential. And, unfortunately, women themselves have often accepted the verdict. Acquiescing in an arbitrarily restricted definition of their capacities, they have made the definition seem true. They have incorporated "an image of the self that paralyzes the will and short circuits the brain, that makes them deny the evidence of their senses and internalize self-doubt to a fearful degree."[38]

Self-awareness and self-assertion can help women overturn this image. But not in the abstract. Women do not live in a social vacuum. Their "selves" are in fact social selves. Awareness of their (systematically patterned and shared) social situation is essential to any meaningful awareness of "self." Likewise, assertiveness must be directed toward changing oppressive social arrangements and values. Mere interpersonal assertiveness can at best provide *ad hoc* improvements in the situations of particular women, often at the expense of others.

As we saw in the earlier example of health foods, when cultural priorities and social patterns are deeply entrenched, advocates of change have to move along many fronts. In areas of overt social and economic discrimination against women—such as employment or the financing of credit—the need to exert focused kinds of pressure and to promote specific changes (in legislation, administrative procedure, how particular institutions are organized and operate, etc.) may be pretty obvious. It is hard to deny, in such cases, that the problems are "external" (social) in nature. However, other more elusive aspects of sexism can easily be misinterpreted as being personal or interpersonal in character. Immersion in self-awareness thinking encourages such misinterpretation, and the accompanying belief in "personal growth" and interpersonal competence as key "solutions."

Take, for example, our cultural preoccupation with women's physical attractiveness. Surely this is a kingpin of sexist thinking and acting. Could we eliminate it? And if so, how? We can dismiss, first off, the argument that this preoccupation is natural—and hence uneliminable. Like so many assertions of naturalness, this one is largely unsupported. We know from historical and cross-cultural studies that idealization and adornment of both sexes have occurred widely, the particular patterns varying according to time and place. Interest in the human body and physical beauty may be natural, but certainly not the uneven obsession with woman's beauty that we display. Quite to the contrary, this obsession is a socially imposed artifact. It reflects and reinforces a specific system of outlooks and behaviors governing relations between the sexes, and defining the "appropriate" roles for women and men.

Throughout her entire lifetime, woman is tyrannized by this cult of physical appearance. She learns even as a very young girl (and boys learn it as well) that what counts for a woman is being beautiful—or at least pretty or attractive. Boys are evaluated on their activity and accomplishments, girls on their appearance. Girls grow up with constant indoc-

trination in the need to beautify themselves. They are surrounded with signs (in the mass media and elsewhere) of the
enormous value society places on female beauty. Women
learn to work on their appearance, to make themselves pleasing to men. Their main "role models" are the glamorous
movie stars and photographers' models, who "teach them
that women are articles of conspicuous consumption in the
male market," that "women are made to be looked at."[39]

Costumers and beautifiers galore cater commercially to the
need to emulate these unrealistically perfect idols. The frantic
recourse to cosmetics, dieting, and enticing attire begins at a
very early age. And it never really ends. The market for cosmetics, for example, seems virtually inexhaustible. If sales
should slack off, manufacturers can always promote a new
beauty "need." Perhaps the best example recently has been
the "feminine hygiene deodorant," another of those items
that somehow people got along perfectly well without in the
past. Idealizing beauty pays well. Since most women cannot
hope to match the ideal models, they can be kept in a state
of permanent insecurity about their looks, and therefore in
permanent need of new and greater efforts. In economic
terms, the demand for beautifiers is inelastic (no price is too
great).

Under this system, women learn too that the reactions men
(and even other women) have to them will be heavily conditioned by their physical appearance. Beginning at an early age,
girls must accustom themselves to a perpetual bombardment
of sexually suggestive looks and comments from unknown
men encountered in the street, the subways, anywhere and
everywhere. A woman alone apparently is always "fair game"
for such treatment—which Ingrid Bengis describes thoroughly
(with frequent reference to "sucking noises" and the like).
To call such behavior "hassling" (a term much used by young
women today) makes it no less demeaning or infuriating.

In both her work and her interpersonal relations, woman
is likewise treated as a decorative and sexual object. Who

would doubt that if a woman were elected President of the United States, newspaper accounts would describe her (if possible) as "an attractive ash blonde." Women's looks are focused on, or at the very least mentioned, no matter what their accomplishments. Women's relations with male work partners invariably are affected, one way or another, by the omnipresent male focus on female attractiveness. This is, of course, a two-edged sword. Men exploit it for sexual gain. Women exploit it for occupational advancement. All too often, women's work itself gets lost in the shuffle. Similarly, it doesn't take women long to learn that their dating and marriage prospects hinge crucially on their physical attractions. As feminist writer Una Stannard points out, women discover that "their looks are a commodity to be bartered in exchange for a man, not only for food, clothing and shelter, but for love. Women learn early that if you are unlovely, you are unloved."[40] The implications of this, Stannard goes on to note, dramatically highlight woman's status as an object. The loveliest women can expect to catch the richest men, and vice versa.

Economist Thorstein Veblen pointed out long ago—in his classic *Theory of the Leisure Class*—that such disabling female accoutrements as corsets and high heels serve the function of demonstrating ability to forgo productive labor. For a man to have as his mate a decorative object shows not only that he has been able to "secure" a lovely companion, but also that he has the financial wherewithal to maintain her in a state of leisure. This economic-prestige "accomplishment" is reciprocal. Woman attains high status by attracting just the sort of man who will treat her as an object. By the same token, attracting such a prized object is a sure sign of the man's excellence.

So, basically, this is an "economic transaction," hence the not-so-farfetched analogy Marxists and others often draw between marriage and prostitution (the main differences being in price and duration). Signs of the "exchange" are clear: the rapid rise in "fortunes" an extraordinarily beautiful but poor woman may be able to achieve; the ability of even unattractive millionaires to obtain glamorous mates. But on both sides, a good start economically helps. Few women can hope realistically to come close to meeting our society's ideal standards of beauty. However, the woman well enough off to be able to stay in good health, get just the right amounts of rest and exercise, and afford a host of cosmetics and other beauty aids, has a distinct advantage. Under the present system, the most likely losers are the poor and the "plain." Given our ideal of (what is invariably) an artificially constructed beauty, the poor are likely to appear, and to remain, unbeautiful.

Beauty, then, is woman's claim to fame. In the wake of this overwhelming theme, it is awfully hard to advance alternative claims. Even more than does her supposedly nurturant nature, the conviction that for woman beauty is enough implies discrediting her active competences. We should recognize, however, that men too are tyrannized by these outlooks. They are under continuous pressure to attract and hold the most glamorous mates. From their standpoint as well as from women's, relations between the sexes become superficial and mutually exploitative. Their general social prestige may rest largely on how well they play this exploiting game. And that prestige, in turn, feeds still further their power to exploit.

It is not hard to guess how self-awareness enthusiasts might tackle this issue. All that is needed, in their view, is that people should stop this kind of role-playing and instead be authentic individuals. Get in touch with themselves and with each other's real feelings. Then they will be able to abandon stereotypes and relate to each other as whole persons. The beauty problem reflects attempts—by both sexes—to meet externally imposed standards rather than simply "to be." People must take charge of themselves. They must get in real touch with, and feel good about, their bodies. Once they do so, the body-insecurities that feed the artificial beauty cult will vanish. Once men and women generally begin to feel good about themselves, in and through themselves, they will move beyond mutual exploitation games to joyous living.

That all sounds good. Certainly it is true that if men and women everywhere could think and act in completely new ways sexist objectification of women might then vanish. But most likely this will not happen in our lifetimes, let alone overnight. Not all the meditation, rapping, exercise regimes, and self-help formulas extant will (even in combination) bring it to pass. Quite simply, the pattern is too deeply imbedded in our outlooks and our ways of interacting. We can see the difficulties all around us. "Liberated" men, who sincerely want to divest themselves of "male chauvinism," straining (often unsuccessfully) to avoid staring lustfully at the un-bra'd breasts of liberated women. "Liberated" women having a hard time denying themselves advantages they know accrue partly from their attractiveness. "Liberated" parents caught between the wish to raise their children without sex-role stereotyping, and the concern that they should turn out "normal."

To overturn outlooks and behavior so deeply ingrained, we need to get at their sources. Hence the concern of the women's movement about dominant patterns of child-rearing. Sex-role stereotyping (as numerous articles have now shown) begins early. Almost from birth, we are systematically taught to believe that boys achieve, girls look nice. Virtually all adult reactions to children are geared to this difference: expressions of approval and disapproval of behavior, selection and direction of children's pastimes and playthings, favored types of clothing, the content of children's stories, and the examples in children's schoolbooks. And the never-ending barrage of TV fare, in which the glamour girl model for women is juxtaposed with the more active pursuits of men.

Sexist acts and attitudes of particular individuals are but symptoms of this deep sexist strain in our culture. If we really want to change this situation, we need to attack directly its institutional groundings. This is why the women's movement is now so busy documenting sexist practices and their effects, and disseminating more accurate information about the true capacities of men and women. The interconnections between the cult of beauty and other aspects of sexism need to be exposed. Parents must be convinced that it is unhealthy to indoctrinate their children in such outlooks. At the same time, efforts to persuade and to elicit assurances of good will only take us so far in promoting significant change. The multimillion dollar cosmetic industry has a heavily vested interest in perpetuating the beauty myth. Greater self-awareness and better communication are not going to eliminate this. Likewise the fashion industry, the mass media, and the advertising agencies, are all significantly involved in the artificial beautification of women. Direct action and public pressure— through economic boycott, legislative or administrative control, or development of nonsexist alternatives—will be necessary if we are to overcome or alter powerful economic interests of this sort.

Frontal and systematic attacks of this sort, aimed at the system's roots, can be supplemented by more individualized efforts. Every rap session that helps break down sexual stereotypes does some good. So does each case of personal unwillingness to accept sexism—be it a woman worker's refusal to be treated as merely decorative, or a counter-hassling of construction workers (or any other leering man) in the street. And if some women and men become more relaxed or feel better about themselves through meditation or yoga, that too could indirectly help the cause. But, as consciousness-raising reveals, the oppression exists on such a scale and in such intricately webbed patterns that no amount of effort on the personal level alone will suffice.

Perhaps I have loaded the argument a bit. The great difficulty in changing the "women's looks" orientation, after all, lies precisely in the fact that it permeates the entire system of institutionalized sexism. In a sense, if we could get rid of it we would be getting rid of sexism altogether. Nonetheless, this is a good example because it illustrates the interlocking nature of oppressive outlooks and structures. It also shows that even those aspects of woman's situation we might be tempted to view as merely attitudinal are in fact closely tied up with the broad value systems and organized institutions of our society. In a way, the woman's beauty issue brings us up against the omnipresent consumer- and commodity-consciousness of modern American society. Treating woman as a commodity, an object of consumption, could be seen as but an instance of this broader pattern. Not surprisingly, Marxist feminists lean toward this argument, asserting that woman-as-object can only be eliminated if we do away with capitalism. (Evidence from the socialist countries, however, is equivocal. Certainly, women there are taken more seriously as productive members of society. They are less likely to be treated merely as decorative objects. At the same time, what socialist planners might call capitalist vestiges of sexism—such as the desire for cosmetics, the lingering appeal of fashion—maintain a disquieting strength.)

Of course, our goal may be not the abolition of interest in physical attractiveness, but rather a greater sex equality in this matter. It is the disproportionate concern with woman's appearance that is especially offensive. However, serious feminists should not wish to see an equalizing of the obsessions presently displayed by men. In the long run, for women to treat men as sex objects would be a most uncertain gain. As we have seen, a new pattern of mutual objectifying and exploitation is a danger implicit in some of the self-awareness efforts. This result, ironically, contrasts sharply with the individualism and humanity awareness advocates seek to advance. It also negates the real spirit of the women's movement, which must run toward freeing women and men from the restrictiveness and unwholesomeness involved in treating each other as objects.

Whatever specific women's issues we choose to confront, the need for systematic and collective effort soon becomes apparent. Woman's potential is indeed her "human potential." Yet such potential "to be" will not exist until artificial limitations on her activity, as well as distortions of her feelings, are eliminated. Self-preoccupation, of the kind frequently implied in the call for greater awareness, has for the most part contributed to keeping women down. It is awareness of her social nature, and her social situation, that can help her to change course.

VI / Therapy More or Less

A Non-Medical Alternative?

Self-awareness. Who needs it? If we are to believe its promoters, everyone does. Precisely what it is that we need, they never fully explain. Nor, as we've seen, do they ever really make clear just what it is they have to offer. Vaguely defined needs and nebulous solutions characterize the entire awareness movement. Like all panaceas, the idea of awareness can never really be pinned down. It is supposed to be more than just feeling good. Awareness techniques are not simply recreation. They are serious, not frivolous. On the other hand, the movement also shies away from the stern medically oriented terminology of conventional therapy. Self-awareness, it seems, is a kind of therapy more or less.

You don't have to be sick to need it. Achieving personal growth is everybody's business. Awareness thinking thrives on the assumption that few of us are growing adequately. That we are out of touch. That we would all benefit from a little awareness enhancing. Most of the new awareness practitioners disagree with both the theory and practice of psychoanalysis. Yet they are similar to the more fervid enthusiasts of that science-art in believing they have a widely applicable key to greater happiness and improved functioning. However much they tend to deny it, they present themselves as the new healers.

In a number of highly provocative books, renegade psychiatrist Thomas Szasz has warned us that his profession is gaining too much power. He claims that mental illness is a "myth," that what psychiatrists usually deal with are actually "problems in living." Such problems are quite different from those of organic illness. Often they are such that psychiatrists have no special competence to handle them. Yet we have looked to psychiatry for answers to all our problems. We hire psychiatrists to take care of situations (and people) we find unmanageable, or even unpleasant. We impose compulsory psychiatric solutions on individuals who can't or won't fit the approved mold. Many of his colleagues, according to Szasz, too readily accept and wield an awesome, and dangerous social power.[1]

The elements of compulsion that loom so large in our recourse to psychiatry lie at the heart of Szasz's objections. His main focus is on the uses of psychiatry by the organized state. Most particularly, he objects to compulsory confinement of the so-called mentally ill. Even leaving aside procedural violations of individual rights that occur in connection with confinement (a good many of which he documents), most compulsory hospitalization he maintains is unnecessary and undesirable. Psychiatrists who act "in the best interests of" the patient, or because of his or her assumed dangerousness (to self or others) are euphemistically rationalizing a questionable curtailment of freedom. By lending themselves to this exercise of social power, psychiatrists depart widely from their legitimate role in a voluntary helping relationship.

Many of the legal uses of psychiatry, Szasz insists, should be replaced by voluntary private help or social services (care of the aged, for example), by less equivocal use of the criminal justice system (when overt criminal acts occur), or by just leaving more people alone (various "deviants"). When we allow psychiatrists to take charge in this way, to make our difficult decisions for us, we abdicate all personal responsibility for how we live. As more and more problems and situations come to be defined as psychiatric in nature, we move ominously in the direction of a benevolent despotism Szasz sees as culminating in "the psychiatric state."

Does the new self-awareness interest provide an alternative that meets such objections? At first glance, it might seem so. Theoreticians of the awareness movement believed they were developing a new conception of human nature, one that broke with the standard psychiatric formulations. Thus Abraham Maslow referred to a "third force" in psychology, and also used the term "Eupsychian network."[2] He saw the newly emerging "humanistic" outlook as rejecting both of the then dominant schools in psychology—Freudian psychoanalysis and behaviorism-experimentalism (out of which grew the conditioning-oriented "behavior therapy").

In this supposedly humanistic alternative, authoritarian distinctions between doctor and patient would have no place. An artificially imposed "detachment" on the part of the therapist also would have to go.[3] Helping relationships would become reciprocal. Helpers too would grow in the process of helping. Indeed, narrow professionalism itself would be broken down in the process. Technical training as a therapist would become less important than empathy, openness and honesty, and a general leadership ability that would enable one to guide the growth process. (In retrospect, the last-named seems to require a large measure of personal charisma.) With this view, it isn't surprising that professionally trained psychologists and therapists such as Maslow, Carl Rogers, and Fritz Perls were quite prepared to accept Buddhists and body enhancers (along with various other "creativity facilitators") as partners in a common quest.

As originally projected, awareness training seems to fall somewhere in between therapy and education (defined in the broadest possible sense). A person was not supposed to have to feel terrible in order to avail himself or herself of it. Wanting to feel "better" was reason enough for trying to become more aware. And as we might suppose, compulsion was abhorrent to the awareness advisors. Only through voluntary participation, could people give themselves over openly, honestly, and fully to the task of self-exploration.

The new self-help movement has badly distorted these original aims. Commercialism has replaced professionalism. Are we really any better off turning to "facilitators" or "trainers" (often themselves self-trained) to help us with our problems, rather than to "therapists." Critics of encounter groups have warned of the dangers. In one intensive study, members of two groups had a psychiatric casualty rate (definite harm occurring as a result of the sessions) of 9.6 percent, compared to none among control subjects. Commenting on such findings, and on anecdotal reports of individuals experiencing serious breakdowns in the course of encountering, Kurt Back has emphasized that "group encounters can have serious effects, even as other interventions on a person's mind and body do."[4] The questionable value of abandoning professionalism is evident also in connection with the currently popular psychological-help books. Many of the authors have professional credentials. Some have extensive clinical experience. Yet they put a new twist on psychological expertise, by insisting that we can all help ourselves *and* that they alone (with their pat prescriptions and empty formulas) can tell us how. Millions of Americans set loose to practice snap therapy on themselves is surely as dismaying a prospect as the expansion of commercial "growth" emporia. Neither of these developments, nor the guru-domination so evident among the Eastern religious and meditation groups, bodes well for the advent of "participatory democracy" in helping relationships.

If the new movement has abandoned most talk of doctors and patients, it's not at all clear what is taking their place. Just plain human beings relating to each other—that would be the insider's probable response. Critics may see it differently. Andrew Malcolm even refers to the "wretched subjects" who take part in encounter sessions.[5] As regards the movement's commercialized forms, it seems quite appropriate to speak of "customers," even of "buyers." On the disseminating side, it is hard not to think in terms of "promoters" and "distributors." As marketplace outlooks come to dominate the scene (how else might we characterize the heavy commercial promotion of psych-help books?), the language of the marketplace replaces the language of healing.

So far at least, these trends are occurring primarily in a context of free choice. Nobody has to go to a growth center. Nobody has to buy a self-help manual. Presumably anyone who does so has good reason, and therefore may benefit. However, as awareness training becomes commonplace in factories and business organizations, prisons and schools (see the next two sections of this chapter), such voluntarism may go by the boards. Workers, prisoners, and schoolchildren are, after all, captive audiences. It is most questionable whether they are truly free to refuse requests to voluntarily participate. Critic Malcolm (discussing the introduction of training groups in various Canadian organizations and government agencies) stresses the vulnerable position of the prospective trainee: "His livelihood, he well knows, depends on his job, and it would not be comfortable for him to oppose for long the insistence on conformity to the Master Plan for Organizational Excellence."[6]

As we've seen, self-awareness thinking (very much in line with Szasz's urgings) does place a heavy emphasis on the individual taking charge, assuming responsibility for his or her own life. Ostensibly this could work against passive reliance on experts, even the new self-awareness ones. Also, awareness gurus want to abandon all determinism—especially the early-childhood dynamic-unconscious determinism that Freudian psychoanalysis stresses. Yet, as our review of awareness thinking should have convinced us, the persisting focus on the individual, and the absence of social content clearly imply a self-enclosed circle of blame. Not only must we *take* responsibility, but in fact we *are* responsible for everything that's happening to us.

Szasz's professed apolitical concern with individual rights can be (and has been) put to conservative uses. His opposition to state uses of psychiatry shades uneasily into condemnation of almost all state action aimed at "helping" people. Awareness enhancers, for their part, do not deny the need for social change so much as they simply avoid that larger arena in their preoccupation with the "growing" self. But at least by implication, the deficiency is again located primarily in individuals. The resulting political tack is essentially (through inaction) a conservative one. As Russell Jacoby insists, "even the most extended therapy remains therapy: a choice in how to treat the individual that leaves untouched the social roots. In that sense there is no such activity as radical therapy— there is only therapy and radical politics."[7]

An interesting attempt to refute this argument has been the formation of "alternative helping centers." The problems such centers have experienced, and the changes they've undergone, illustrate the difficulty of fusing self-awareness thinking and social action. Often begun (in the late 1960s) as psychological first-aid stations for "street people" (drug crisis centers, "crash pads," "hotlines," and the like), these centers now seem to be moving in the direction of becoming more comprehensive counseling agencies. At the outset, they were staffed almost entirely by volunteers—mainly middle-class college students and graduates who had been influenced by both counterculture politics and social critiques of conventional psychotherapy. Organizers of the centers hoped to challenge dominant social and political values, and at the same time implement a self-awareness orientation. Gordon Holleb and Walter Abrams, founders of Pequod, an alternative counseling program in Cambridge, Massachusetts, note that the new centers emphasized "learning through personal experience." Potential group leaders for the alternative programs "would always begin by being a participant in the kind of counseling group that he later would lead. Consciousness raising about political and sexual issues was considered an important part of training. The basic tenet of alternative training was that self-awareness and empathy with the client are essential to being a competent counselor."[8]

Alternative centers would try to break down the distinctions between staff and client. They would provide free, nonjargonized help, in a pleasant, informal, nonbureaucratized setting. Alternative helpers would be "sensitive, open people with a minimum of formal training and no degrees in psychology." Programs would emphasize group, rather than individual, counseling and would have the "personal growth" of staff members (as well as of clients) as a major goal. Alternative helping was to emphasize "change not adjustment" and would try "to include an understanding of the political and social roots of individual problems within the counseling."[9]

Holleb and Abrams provide a revealing account of the ambivalences, obstacles, and other growing pains experienced by several of these organizations. An original notion of building an "open trusting community" in which staff and clients would participate equally had to give way. Instead the centers were transformed "into service organizations with clear distinctions between staff and client." Local clinicians began to become involved in the programs, and early staff members themselves sought advanced training. Interpersonal, organizational, and financial difficulties had to be dealt with. Problems arose concerning the payment of staff and the charging of fees (another undesired step toward which the centers

moved). Concern was felt that the efforts of untrained counselors to achieve their own personal growth might dilute or
impair their helping of others.

Perhaps most significant of all was the need to face up to
the "reality . . . that the organization was not involved in
major social change. It had never successfully defined what
that social change was to be, beyond supporting alternative
life styles and creating a community between helpers and
clients." This comment, describing one of the specific programs, appears to apply to the centers generally. As Holleb
and Abrams note, with some exceptions (mainly the provision
in several centers of special gay and feminist counseling),
"The majority of staffs at alternative centers fail to actively
include a social perspective within the counseling." Inability
to develop this once hoped-for political element is not surprising, given the overriding personal growth orientation of
center members. To their credit, the centers seem for the
most part (in the face of considerable temptation) to have
avoided being "co-opted" by the "mental health establishment." Some have resisted bureaucratization in favor of "collective" organization. But the awareness–trust interpersonal
skill themes have remained dominant. Characteristically,
when members want to examine their collective situation and
progress, they go off somewhere on a "retreat." Such sessions
"put people back in personal contact with one another." They
symbolize "the realization that the way people communicate
with one another in a work setting is as important to good
services as individual experience or training."[10]

In criticizing establishment psychiatry, Szasz has stressed
the tendency toward therapeutic overreach. People's willingness to bring their problems to psychiatrists is matched by the
latter's willingness to try to solve all manner of problems.
Evaluative elements built into the process of diagnosis are
glossed over, as more and more types of behavior are seen to
be pathological. Radicalism, "dropping out," and poor school
performance, as well as drug use, homosexuality, and prostitu-

tion become grist for the psychiatric mill. Some psychological helpers seem quite prepared to consider any and every "problem in living" a psychological one—be it racism or poverty, or low job morale.

Alternative helping centers that make a special effort to avoid judging people may not fall into this trap. Yet the claims for self-awareness, like psychiatric claims, are loosely expandable. True, awareness advisors do not label people "sick," merely lacking in awareness and deficient in crucial interpersonal skills, out of touch and therefore not experiencing real joy. They are continuously telling us how empty our lives are, a prophecy that easily becomes self-fulfilling. At the very least, as we've seen, they present to us (especially in the glib self-help manuals) a highly inadequate conception of unhappiness—and hence of happiness as well. When root causes are ignored, prescriptions for the ailment founder.

Given its simplistic approach to social change, awareness thinking easily takes the jump from prescribing for the individual to prescribing for the world. Thus proponents of transcendental meditation tell us that if people all over the world practice TM, the collective result will go well beyond their feeling better and functioning more effectively. "A global qualitative improvement in all aspects of individual life must lead to a parallel improvement in all aspects of the social environment, including the design of social institutions."[11] If one can make far-reaching claims of this sort then one is likely to find with ease awareness answers to myriad specific social problems and conditions: international tension and conflict, race prejudice and discrimination, industrial discontent, crime and delinquency, drug addiction, you name it. Whatever the situation about which people feel "something must be done," the new specialists claim to be capable of handling it.

Some of this optimism derives from the movement's long experience with sensitivity "training groups" (T-groups) for business organizations.[12] This activity has been central to the work of the National Training Laboratory in Bethel, Maine,

and several other major encounter-group centers that helped
lay much of the groundwork for the present awareness movement. Corporate interest in awareness techniques continues
to boom. In organizational circles, sensitivity training for
executives (either through enrollment in one of the centers
or through some in-house program) is now often thought of
as standard operating procedure. Apparently corporations are
susceptible to the newer versions of awareness-enhancing as
well. Current books on meditation cite long lists of important
organizations in which this practice is favored, if not imposed.
Similarly, a recent account notes that, "Huge corporations
like Martin Marietta are already looking into biofeedback as
a way to stimulate creativity and reduce anxiety in top-level
executives."[13] No doubt yoga and bioenergetics have their
corporate devotees too. Psych-help popularizers are drawn to
the business bandwagon, frequently citing the success stories
of "prominent business executives" who have adopted their
particular approach.

Although some of these recent fads may be short-lived, the
training-group procedures seem to have proven themselves
over time—at least to the satisfaction of corporate leaders.
They are built around the themes of improving communication, and developing interpersonal skills. And they are
grounded in substantial social science research on such topics
as small-group behavior, organizational structure and dynamics, and "human relations in industry" (the importance
of "the human factor" in affecting productivity and morale).
They aim at enhancing "organizational effectiveness," by
cutting through the barriers to communication that become
entrenched through formal hierarchies and established rules.
If the organizational members can openly and honestly confront their problems, this will improve collaboration and coordination. It will also give them a more meaningful sense of
participation in a common endeavor. Rapping and role-playing, exercises in problem-solving, and efforts to reveal the
organization's covert tensions and informal patterns, will

improve the organization and at the same time help the particular individuals. They will become better leaders and managers, more effective in their interpersonal relations.

How much desired change encounter sessions actually produce is uncertain. Reviewing almost a hundred evaluation studies (of varying sorts), Kurt Back found the evidence of real change to be quite inconclusive. In early evaluations, there often was no comparison with a "control group" (a similar group not undergoing the training). In many studies, "change" was assessed during the group sessions themselves, with no adequate follow-up. Usually the reports of change came from the trainees themselves, rather than through ratings by outside observers or objective measures of performance outside the group setting. As Back notes, these procedures should encourage positive findings, so the fact that the evidence of change they produced is mixed takes on even stronger significance. He refers also to an apparent "built-in resistance against accepting negative evidence. After a deep experience of this kind, one wants to believe that some change occurred."[14]

As I mentioned earlier, these methods may carry some specific danger for psychologically unstable or vulnerable individuals. But more likely they do little harm. They do perpetuate a view of the organization that—while in some respects highly sophisticated—too glibly assumes the wonders that better communicating and other supposedly content-free skills can produce. They may imply a nonexistent ability to relate away real conflicts within the organization, or to ignore events or forces outside it. And they may become a device by which top management seeks to quiet challenges from below to organizational goals or procedures. Yet if the basic idea is to teach executives that they have to pay attention to human relations—and in the process to pay such attention to the executives themselves—the sensitizing may well do some good.

However, this provides no sound model for applying self-awareness approaches in other (nonorganizational) realms.

Although they are not really self-enclosed systems, organizations have a more or less circumscribed structure and clear focus that are absent in many other situations awareness prescribers confront. They are indeed more manageable than are the "problems" or patterns of behavior that spread across an entire society (or the world—as in the case of international conflict). Organizations have specific goals, in terms of which (once they have been accepted) it may be possible to assess "effectiveness." They may incorporate common interests and a working consensus to a degree absent in many other situations. Likewise there is an element of "legitimate authority" built into the organizational structure that gives the organizational arena a unique character.

Finally, sensitivity training in corporations at times may focus on quite specific organizational problems: a certain work team is not displaying team work, a particular echelon of management seems always to be at loggerheads with another, a given procedural innovation shows signs of backfiring, supervisors have low morale, and so on. This highlights a point of importance regarding awareness-enhancing in general. Such efforts are most likely to have real meaning when they are directed at a specific problem or task, and when they are limited to techniques appropriate for that purpose. Trying to improve morale in a particular work group in a given organization is a far cry from trying to make people in general happy. Then too, the problems of an organization may lend themselves to some of the available awareness methods. *Some* of the problems of organizations (and indeed *some* of the problems of relationships) may in fact be problems of communication. If awareness facilitators would limit their goals and claims, and match technique to problem, it would be much easier to be optimistic about the results.

Emphasizing communication does seem to be one of the more useful awareness ideas. It can be given a specific focus for "healing" purposes much easier than some of the amorphous ideas about the real "self." Of course, supposedly all of these notions are intertwined—good communication means being open, responding to feelings, developing trust, etc., etc. But if anything in this theoretical mishmash really works, it probably is the opportunity direct communication provides to clear up misunderstandings and to appreciate the other person's point of view. Again, however, this can only solve problems that center around communication difficulty. The further we get beyond anything approximating a neatly circumscribed "closed system," the less likely it is that most problems will be of that sort.

We can see this in a number of other areas of application. As I emphasized earlier, the idea of open marriage may (among other shortcomings) exaggerate the importance of communication. Nonetheless, it seems obviously useful that marriage partners should talk to each other. Not all marriage problems can be solved through better communication, but usually some can. This belief has now crystallized in a quite substantial "marriage encounter" movement. According to one account, this movement (which is also religious in orientation—and in the New York metropolitan area includes Roman Catholic, Jewish, and Episcopal contingents) has attracted 175,000 couples to its weekend encounter sessions. As well as voluntary religious services, and talks by clergymen and encounter veterans, these weekends feature "working sessions during which partners write each other letters on suggested topics (for example: 'What are the qualities that most attracted me to you?'), then exchange letters and dialogue in private about the answers."[15] It seems clear that this variant on awareness exercises can do little harm. It may help some marriages. Needless to say, it leaves completely untouched the broader sociocultural context that shapes the relationships (including marriages) between particular men and women.

Another area in which rapping may have special usefulness is that of interracial attitudes. Naturally, attitudes and feelings about racial issues may often come to the fore in any encounter-group meeting or rap session. But by now there have been a great many sessions explicitly set up for that purpose. Some have been widely broadcast on radio or television. Commenting on one such encounter (a twenty-two-hour nonstop session in 1969 convened by a Boston radio station and including some key leaders of both the black and white communities), writer Jane Howard asserts: "In a space seventeen by seventeen feet, over a period of nearly a full day, the barriers were assaulted. It turned out that the blacks and whites eventually could see each other as individuals, unconnected with their official roles."[16]

Encounter techniques have special pertinence in this area because many of our attitudes and feelings on racial matters are so heavily built up around misunderstandings and stereotypes. That favorable change might occur through direct confrontation seems supported by the "contact hypothesis" sociologists advance. Findings in research on people who have moved from segregated to integrated situations (for example, in interracial housing projects or in the army) often show that increased personal contact with people of the other race leads to increasingly favorable attitudes toward them. However, if interracial encounters are promoted primarily for their emotional catharsis effect, they could well backfire. Noting that "marathon groups between whites and blacks often reach the point of expressing strong hostilities and recognizing many hostile feelings," sociologist Kurt Back considers it an open question whether such highly emotional encounters "may add fuel to the fire or may be a technique to control potentially festering conflicts."[17]

Even where effective this approach touches merely the individuals involved. Neither the institutionalized sources of racial attitudes, nor the broad structures that shape the relative situations of blacks and whites, are affected. Interracial problems have many aspects that simply cannot be reduced to the arena of direct interpersonal contact. As a result these direct-contact techniques have at most a limited value. This limitation is even more blatantly apparent in schemes for applying awareness thinking in the international sphere. There, the complexities are vastly greater and the proposals seem even more simpleminded.

International conflicts in part reflect tensions that could theoretically be released in other ways, and communication failures or misunderstandings. But these represent only a minute part of the melange of factors setting country against country. Historical, economic, cultural, ideological, and political differences and clashes cannot be obliterated by statesmen getting more in touch and "leveling" with each other. These conflicts of values and interests are quite real and very persistent. They're not just the result of emotional blockages and gaps in communicating. Yet psychologist–encounter theorist Carl Rogers envisions what he himself terms a "fantasy"—a kind of international rap session to mend the breach between two nations. Unofficial delegations of citizens "could meet together as persons, not as representatives of set points of view." Though their initial exploration would be tension-filled, out of it "would come an increasing number of insights and a much deeper understanding of each other's point of view and the reasons for it. Ideally, the facilitator for this group should be a trained person belonging to neither country."[18]

Such efforts, again, could have some value—but of a necessarily limited kind. Informal diplomacy has always occurred. Intentional cross-national meetings not too dissimilar to that proposed by Rogers have been convened (for example the Pugwash conferences on disarmament). Where the focus is clear, and overriding common interests pronounced, such sessions may be productive. However, there is no reason at all to believe that some new type of encountering will erase international conflicts. As I've already mentioned, the expectations of other kinds of awareness advisers—such as meditation enthusiasts—are even more fanciful. No amount of meditating is going to "take care of" the Middle East, U.S.–Soviet relations, or Hindu–Muslim conflicts. It is all very well for the

Maharishi to tell us that, "The basis of peace is bliss."[19] Unfortunately, bliss is not enough. While we individually seek it, events march on.

The Deviant and the Disadvantaged

The new healers do somewhat better when they try to tackle problems in which conventional therapists had already shown strong interest. Here, there is a substantial tradition of focusing on the "deviating" individual. A good example is drug addiction. To want to "treat" drug users at all may be ironic, given the part that psychedelic drugs have played in generating awareness outlooks. Disseminators of these outlooks, however, actually display a variety of attitudes toward, and beliefs about, drugs. And with respect to hard-core (opiate) addiction, there have been some serious awareness-oriented treatment efforts.

Some of the new helpers believe that once people get really in tune with themselves, and rid themselves of general tensions, they will no longer turn to drugs. This notion of the new awareness as a technique for preventing drug use is loosely stated and not much supported by hard data. For Arthur Janov, drug use and addiction represent efforts to ward off the "primal pains." Since the "post-primal" no longer has compulsions, a person who has gone through Janov's new therapy would presumably have no need of drugs.[20] The basic idea here is tension-release. Similarly, the authors of the book *TM* attribute drug use to underlying psychological tension. By restoring equilibrium, and promoting general feelings of well-being, meditation "may well offer a plausible solution for all forms of drug abuse."[21] They cite various studies indicating low rates of drug use among meditators. Several of these, however, involved drinking and marijuana use rather than hard-core narcotics. Since these practices, along with meditation, might be seen simply as alternative ways of spending free time, the meaning of such findings is uncertain. A person who spends a lot of time meditating, will invariably spend less time drinking or smoking pot. Whether personal tensions that relate to drug use have really been alleviated remains an open question.

The most solid application of awareness thinking in the drug field grew out of the encounter-group tradition. It has not been aimed at the general prevention of drug taking. Rather, it has involved developing a technique and an environment through which addicts who want to "kick the habit" can stay off drugs. The prototype of this approach is Synanon.[22] Begun in 1958 as a small residential program for addicts and alcoholics (located in a single house in southern California), Synanon has spread rapidly. Jane Howard reports that the organization now "controls $7 million worth of real estate. It has branches in five California cities . . . as well as in New York City, Detroit, and San Juan, Puerto Rico. Its 'life-style,' dispensed through 80 groups called Tribes, is based on a kind of encounter group known as the Synanon Game."[23]

Synanon games involve freewheeling discussion sessions that are sometimes described as a kind of "attack therapy." Members tell their own stories, under strong group pressure to be open and honest—especially about their problems and personal failings. A no-holds-barred dissection of each person's deficiencies is encouraged. But strong group support of determined members is provided as well. Keeping free of drugs is a cardinal rule. Heavy emphasis is placed on developing anti-drug attitudes and positive social values. Although critics have condemned Synanon practices for incorporating what they saw as a merciless attack on members' self-respect, morale in the organization has always been high and considerable success in keeping members off drugs has been achieved. Enthusiasts insist that "seeming verbal brutality can be an act of love in disguise."[24]

At least in its early days, a large part of Synanon's success lay in social-system aspects of its program. The new member

came to Synanon House eager to kick the habit, and did so
with warm support from the residents—who had all been
through the same thing themselves. He or she joined a new,
drug-free community. Within the organization there was a
system of graded work roles, with members gradually taking
on positions of greater responsibility. This gave them both
meaningful work (partly for the organization itself, but Synanon set up outside "businesses" as well), and a new basis for
developing favorable self-conceptions. Some critics saw this
as being more of a protective community than a therapeutic
one—since the most successful members seemed to stay within
the organization itself rather than "graduating" to a full life
in the outside world. Dependence on Synanon was substituted
for dependence on drugs. But there is no gainsaying that, one
way or another, the program has kept a good many former
addicts off drugs for considerable periods of time.

Synanon was the beginning of the entire "therapeutic community" approach to treating addicts. Programs of this sort,
usually run at least in part by ex-addicts, have proliferated
rapidly. In the New York City area, Odyssey House, Phoenix
House, and Daytop Village are probably just some of the
better-known organizations employing these techniques. Daniel Casriel, a psychiatrist who was an early enthusiast of Synanon, later a director of Daytop, and who now (interestingly)
runs a more general personal growth program in New York,
nicely conveys the awareness themes this approach embodies.
He sees as a major causal factor in addiction, "the *inability to
communicate emotionally*, which directly leads to a void in
which chemicals become a substitute for human feelings,
emotional pleasure: love."[25] When encounter-type sessions in
these programs do help former addicts to remain abstinent, the
heavy focus on drug problems and developing antidrug outlooks may be one of the main reasons. The guidance and support for dealing with specific life problems that the programs
offer undoubtedly help too.

Unfortunately, advocates of the encounter and therapeutic

community approach often tend to see their scheme as *the* unquestionable answer to all addiction problems. They develop vested interests and condemn what might be complementary programs. In the early days, the leaders of Synanon (whose success has in large measure reflected the personal charisma of founder "Chuck" Dederich) even insisted that only its own members were competent to run real Synanon-type sessions. The organization became defensive, if not paranoid, about criticism. According to supporter-chronicler Lewis Yablonsky, "The sheer existence of the Synanon approach is considered by some professionals to be an attack upon the *status quo* and vested interest of their professional domain. Synanon's position that some of its 'patients' can become therapists seems to draw fire from many professional quarters."[26]

That was written in the early days of the therapeutic communities. The approach now receives considerable public support. We know also that today the self-help orientation to which Yablonsky refers is much more respectable. What has not changed, however, is that rap sessions and the reshaping of former addicts' outlooks (even when effective) can only begin to alter the many-faceted drug-addiction situation. These methods for voluntary treatment of the already addicted affect neither the root causes of turning to addictive drugs, nor the secondary aspects of the addiction situation we have fostered through our repressive drug policies. Some people become addicts because of tension, but more often than not the causes of the tension are objectively clear and remediable through social action. The average ghetto-dwelling addict (notwithstanding middle-class drug problems, heroin addicts remain concentrated in the ghettos) needs decent housing and jobs more than rapping and meditation.[27] Inadequate medical care causes tension. So do rats in the bedroom. Individualized "tension-release" methods may help some people who already suffer from a drug habit. But they should not deflect attention from these broad socioeconomic dimensions of the problem.

Another striking limitation of awareness approaches in this area is the failure to confront such policy-escalated features as the illicit traffic and addict-crime. Punitive narcotics laws create and uphold the economic incentives underlying the black market in drugs. As the late Herbert Packer, a legal scholar, pointed out, "Regardless of what we think we are trying to do, if we make it illegal to traffic in commodities for which there is an inelastic demand, the actual effect is to secure a kind of monopoly profit to the entrepreneur who is willing to break the law."[28] Given the widespread and compelling demand, and the fact that drug transactions occur between willing buyers and sellers, legislative attempts to curb the spread of drugs are for all practical purposes unenforceable. They keep the price of drugs (almost worthless in themselves) high, and ensure the addict's need to commit money-producing crimes to support his or her habit. Most disinterested observers believe this process accounts for a very large proportion of all crimes against property.[29]

A desire to undercut the economic incentives to trafficking and eliminate the financial pressures impelling addict criminality underlies the interest American specialists have shown in British drug policy. Although the British approach of legally prescribing heroin for existing addicts at low cost has not worked perfectly, neither is it the "failure" that sensationalist American news accounts and statements by punitively minded law-enforcers have sometimes tried to suggest. Despite some recent increases in the number of addicts, the fact remains that provision of low-cost opiates has greatly inhibited illicit traffic, and addict-crime continues to be negligible.[30] A similar attempt to reduce the secondary aspects of the drug problem is the development of methadone maintenance programs. A recent federal court ruling upholding employment rights of ex-addicts currently in such programs, noted that "a person maintained on a constant dose of methadone can perform normally by every standard that relates to employability, and . . . except in rare cases, there are no side effects making such a person incapable of being employed."

Nor do such persons have any need to commit crimes in order to obtain drugs. Commenting with approval on this ruling, *The New York Times* pointed out that in New York City alone there are now approximately 40,000 ex-heroin addicts being legally maintained on this (addicting, but not disabling) drug.[31]

Even this sketchy look at some of the complexities of the drug problem makes clear the gross oversimplification involved in seeing self-awareness as a comprehensive solution. Again, it may be true that if all people in our society could be free of all tensions (and, we should add, justified grievances) such problems would never arise. However, looking the other way (in this case, inward) will not cause the socio-economic and legal ramifications to disappear. Until our society is a very different one, being our own best friends will not suffice. The same kinds of points could be made with respect to the movement's glib pronouncements on crime and delinquency. Here too, the focus is on tension-release and greater in-touchness for the individual, to the almost complete exclusion of the social aspects of criminality. Awareness prescribers never come to grips with the old and wise dictum that "a society gets the criminals it deserves."

We have already seen how "reality therapy"—with its particularly strong responsibility theme—comes down hard on the "delinquent." People break the law because they are irresponsible. Many of the general self-help books might lead us to the same kind of conclusion. With their constant references to taking charge of oneself, to not blaming the "system" or other people (not being a "grievance collector," as Greenwald puts it), they reinforce a tendency to which we already are excessively prone: finding the alleged "causes" of crime in personal deficiency. Thomas Harris describes "I'm OK—You're Not OK" as the "criminal position."[32] This outlook, which he attributes to childhood brutalization, is found among incorrigible offenders—"criminal psychopaths." It is a result of "stroking deprivation," and presumably will respond (if at all) to some kind of compensatory stroking. He may well be right, but even if he is this cannot get us very far in our efforts to ameliorate crime problems in general.

The money-producing "hustles" that abound in our ghettos, professional theft, "white-collar" and corporate crimes, and Watergate-type crimes—these patterns cannot be explained in such terms. Nor indeed can many violent crimes, which often are crimes of passion or otherwise occur among people who knew each other beforehand. Criminology has long floundered in its use of the "psychopath" diagnosis, which most experts now recognize as a "wastebasket category" into which are dumped many of the offenders who don't fit other psychodiagnostic formulations. Even if there are "psychopaths" (and not all specialists are convinced of this), they commit but a tiny fraction of existing crimes.[33]

According to Maharishi Mahesh Yogi, crime and delinquency are due to a "weak mind," a condition that can easily be remedied. With the release of tension through deep meditation, "the hard and cruel nature of man changes to one of tolerance and compassion." Accordingly, he advocates widespread institutions of meditation for the "speedy and effective" rehabilitation of criminals and delinquents.[34] Likewise, his disciples who authored the book *TM* refer to several studies of the effects on prisoners of meditation. They emphasize the quick and inexpensive nature of this "rehabilitation" technique, and report pronounced reductions in stress and anxiety levels among the meditators. Such methods (which should be on a voluntary basis) will help us to eliminate crime, because criminality is due to the individual's inability to find acceptable means of fulfilling personal needs.[35] Apparently, these TM boosters assume that decreased anxiety levels in prison will carry over automatically to produce happy and productive lives on the outside. There is no reason whatsoever to believe this. It goes without saying that they ignore completely the need to provide post-release guidance and adequate job opportunities for ex-prisoners. Nor do they seem concerned with the problems posed by an offender's return to the former (often criminogenic) environment and patterns of association. These are among the major reasons other rehabilitation schemes fail. Meditating in prison (and afterwards) may contribute to post-release adjustment, but clearly it won't be enough.

Prison officials, however, appear ready to try anything that might work. A recent news account, for example, reported an extensive program of "awareness training" instituted at the Kansas State Penitentiary, under the sponsorship (it's interesting to note) of the National Alliance of Businessmen. In addition to inmate–staff sensitivity sessions, "The prison has also undertaken classes in yoga, transcendental meditation, transactional analysis . . . drama, music, painting and horticulture."[36] As this suggests, rehabilitators (whose past record has been so dismal) try frantically to be "innovative." Actually, however, there is quite a long history of (relatively successful) use of encounterlike group-treatment methods in correctional institutions. A good many of the more effective programs for treating juvenile offenders have centered around "guided group interaction" or some other version of this approach.[37] These adaptations of the encounter idea usually emphasize ideas and values every bit as much as feelings. Often the programs feature as well group members working in the outside community. And the focused nature of the sessions enables members to deal with the specific problems that led to their delinquency and that face them now.

Similarly, efforts to establish Synanon-type schemes in prisons for adults appear to have met with some success.[38] One encounter-tradition technique that may be especially helpful in prisons and in the criminal-justice system generally, is "roleplaying." Placing yourself in the other person's situation greatly increases your understanding of his or her feelings and reactions. Role-playing may break down stereotypes and misunderstandings that influence the relations between prisoners and guards. Likewise, there have been some experiments in which criminal-court judges voluntarily went to jail. This may well increase empathy, but the fact remains that such role-reversal is contrived and temporary. The judge continues to do the sentencing, the offender is the one who is sentenced. The inmate can't get out, the guard can.

As in the case of addiction, awareness approaches at best constitute a supplement to more conventional after-the-fact treatment efforts. They make no significant inroads on the basic societal conditions that breed crime in the first place. Even such a conservative body as the President's Crime Commission asserted in its 1967 Report that "unless society does take concerted action to change the general conditions and attitudes that are associated with crime, no improvement in law enforcement and administration of justice . . . will be of much avail."[39] Some individuals, who come to feel better about themselves, might not commit some offenses that otherwise might occur. That's the most we can say for the new techniques. The criminogenic values so prevalent in American life (material success at all costs, moral corner cutting, etc.) are never really directly attacked through self-awareness efforts. They are downgraded and vaguely condemned in some of the movement's proclamations. Awareness gurus favor alternative values, yet the preoccupation with feelings and process, the lack of interest in social forms and content, ensure that current value systems will remain in force—largely untouched.

This failure to confront the groundings of criminality is even more striking with respect to objective socioeconomic features of our system that encourage crime. Crime occurs at all levels in our society—a fact highlighted by Watergate. But virtually all disinterested experts recognize important links between serious street crime and the persistence of substantial poverty and racial discrimination. Michael Harrington noted, in his already classic exposé of poverty, *The Other America*, that "the city jail is one of the basic institutions of the other America. Almost everyone whom I encountered in the 'tank'

was poor: skid-row whites, Negroes, Puerto Ricans."[40] Our
system of criminal justice tends to split along racial lines.
Predominantly white police patrol predominantly black lower-
class neighborhoods. Predominantly white lawyers and judges
"process" predominantly black offenders. White correctional
officers "guard" black inmates. The socioeconomic conditions
underlying this situation have changed little since the Kerner
Commission (appointed to examine the summer 1967 riots in
various U.S. cities) warned of a deep reservoir of legitimate
grievances in our black population. During a period of economic recession the situation, if left alone, can only worsen.

Our high crime rates will not be greatly reduced until the
basic inequities that support them are removed. Approaching
crime problems in self-awareness terms simply reinforces the
tendency I have described elsewhere as "compartmentalizing
crime."[41] We are unwilling to recognize how closely criminality is woven into the very fabric of our system. We persist in
seeing it as something done *to* society, rather than in society.
The "criminal," then, must be some quite different kind of
human being. Evil or sick, or perhaps—in line with awareness
outlooks—irresponsible because of unallayed personal tensions. Either way, we pin the responsibility on the individual,
rather than on the system that brought him (or her) into
being.

At the same time, we lose sight of the invariable political
element in crime situations. "Crime" is a way of defining behavior through legal enactment. In a sense, we create crimes
by making laws. It is possible to argue, then, that we have
been imposing the wrong definitions, creating and attacking
the wrong crimes.[42] The possibility is underlined by the radical's assertion that "all prisoners are political prisoners." We
sense it when we recognize our patent failure to take seriously
white-collar and corporate offenses. We confront another
side of it in the argument over "decriminalizing" marijuana
use, homosexual acts, gambling, or prostitution. Because
awareness outlooks focus our attention on individual feelings,

and lead us away from substantive issues of social policy and value choice, they promote neglect of this crucial crime-defining process.

One area in which the debate over crime-defining has become heated, and which also continues to be a major concern of conventional psychotherapists, is homosexuality. This is a type of "deviance" about which the new healers don't say very much. They tend, after all, to be tolerant of "alternative life-styles"—a characterization that appeals to many in the gay community. The more depth-oriented awareness-healers (such as Janov) do see homosexuality as a substitute for true sexuality, and as requiring treatment. ("Post-primals" seem to lose these "unreal" impulses, even persons who before were overtly homosexual.) Assertiveness trainers, emphasizing as we've seen the conditioning of behavior, are inclined to be rather sanguine regarding the possibilities for converting homosexuals to heterosexuality. (If they want to convert. The key point in the assertiveness literature is that you can be whatever you want to be, or at least almost.)

Typically, however, self-awareness schemes do not purport to "treat" homosexuality. On the contrary, the general outlook they reflect stresses "openness" to a variety of experiences, including sexual ones. If it feels good, it's okay. In some awareness-influenced circles, you aren't truly liberated if you haven't tried a little of everything. Critics sometimes make the mistake of considering this invitation to widened experiencing as a serious threat to heterosexuality, if not to the stability of the whole family system. Behind this misunderstanding lurks the strange belief that if the floodgates are not shut fast, we will all become homosexuals. Thus George Gilder warns us that "It is crucial to affirm precarious males in their heterosexuality."[43]

Recently the American Psychiatric Association removed homosexuality from its standard list of psychological illnesses. Yet the label of pathology dies hard. Psychiatrists continue to insist that persons who say they have accepted themselves

as homosexuals and are satisfied with that orientation are trying to "deal with pain by denying it exists" and that neither
"assertions of gay pride nor psychiatric declarations have the
power to make homosexuals feel proud or happy."[44] It isn't
possible in this brief discussion to deal with the thorny issue
of whether a homosexual orientation inevitably implies unhappiness or emotional conflict. (Though we may note in
passing that some studies of nonpatient homosexuals have
revealed no unusual amount of "pathology" when their psychological test results were assessed "blind"—by evaluators
who didn't know they were homosexual—and compared with
results for "matched" nonhomosexuals.) Our main concern
here is with self-awareness and its implications.

Some observers see the "new consciousness" as having significantly contributed to gay self-acceptance and militancy.
Dennis Altman, an eloquent interpreter of the homosexual's
situation, states that "When gay liberationists proclaim 'We
are going to be who we are,' they are echoing the mood of the
broader counter-culture."[45] Yet notwithstanding the credo
of "doing your own thing," turning inward for self-awareness
purposes seems likely (on balance) to blunt, rather than encourage, political action. And political action is what homosexuals (collectively) need—regardless of any decisions by
gay individuals either to try to get themselves more "in touch"
with their feelings, or to seek professional counseling of one
sort or another.

Even most critics of gay militancy condemn the legal repression and extensive discrimination with which homosexuals
must contend. Here, much as in the case of the women's
movement, focused group sessions (gay consciousness-raising?) and training in self-assertion may be useful links between self-awareness thinking and real social change. But
"out of the closets and into the growth center" is no substitute for the militant rallying cry "out of the closets and into
the streets." Gay pride is important, but so is gay power. Accounts of the gay liberation struggle show that it has been

hindered (again mirroring the women's movement) by internal factionalism, and by uncertain linkages with potentially supportive movements (women, blacks, etc.). There are important differences of opinion within the gay community. One finds there a broad range of political leanings, attitudes toward accommodation and militancy, views of psychiatry, and exposure to self-awareness ideas and techniques. However, gay liberationists are agreed that social-political action against repressive laws and institutions is a central component of the homosexual cause.[46]

As we have seen, this kind of action requires organization and pressure on a broad front. Here again, the targets are many—including laws, the media, our educational institutions, and public attitudes generally. Gay lobbying, media monitoring, and reeducation efforts already are resulting in less repressive laws, more reasonable programming policies, and decreased public stereotyping of homosexuals. Other needed changes call for comparable effort. Identifying collective interests, asserting collective will. Content-free skill training and unfocused self-searching are only likely to divert homosexuals from mounting the systematic campaign their situation demands.

When we turn from people frequently labeled deviant to those who are more apt to be termed disadvantaged, the self-awareness message shifts from ambiguous to nonexistent. Neither the gurus nor the self-help guides indicate a means to overturn poverty—unless we count their vague intimations that personal fulfillment will mysteriously produce a new and better way of life. Institutionalized racism they similarly ignore. Their only concrete suggestion for helping blacks and other minorities is to change individual attitudes through the new openness and honesty. Surely it's not necessary any longer to document the fact that blacks (along with Puerto Ricans, Chicanos, American Indians) need a great deal more than this. That they need an even break. That the poor need money. That whichever basic life-supporting institutions we examine—housing, education, jobs, health care—systematic disadvantage prevails. That what Michael Harrington so well described as "the vicious circle of poverty" persists: slum living and bad diets lead to sickness; under bad health care, sickness persists; wages and jobs are lost, and hence any chance to pay for better food, housing, and medical care.[47]

As we have seen, you would never believe—from what the awareness advisers have to say—that there are people who have problems of this kind. When they refer to the pains of living they mean something considerably more benign than hunger pains. The personal crises they cite tend to involve difficulties in "relating" or perhaps the dilemma of whether to choose more "creative" work—not the problems of coping with unemployment. Their characteristically glib optimism and touting of personal responsibility reflect either ignorance or avoidance of the built-in barriers to "taking charge" that make life for so many Americans a constant struggle just to survive. Increasingly we see around us a dismaying juxtaposition of a contentment-oriented inner quest and a quite abysmal outer reality. When *The New York Times Magazine* recently published an enthusiastic account of "Tuning Down with TM," it backed directly on the article, "Down and Out in America—In anger and sadness, people in Buffalo tell the story of unemployment."[48]

For white middle-class citizens to become complacently self-preoccupied while their less fortunate fellow Americans struggle and starve is criminal enough. But if the poor or other seriously disadvantaged were themselves to accept the awareness message, that would be the sheerest folly. From the standpoint of advancing their clear collective interests, concentrating individual energies on developing interpersonal skills and inner serenities (both quite desirable, if they could be attained) would only prove counterproductive. Various programs and strategies for ending poverty and racism have been proposed. Yet implementation continues to be piecemeal and inadequate. Planning and forceful advocacy, attain-

ing and using positions of community power, lobbying for
systematic increases in opportunity, and direct confrontations
(demonstrations, rent strikes, flooding the welfare roles, and
the like) will be necessary if the current balance of power and
advantage is to be altered.⁴⁹ Efforts to become "authentic"
will not provide the poor or discriminated against with decent
jobs, housing, or food. Indeed one cannot, in any true sense,
be authentic until those prerequisites have been met.

Other "minorities" in our society that would do well to
resist being seduced by awareness outlooks include the young
and the old. To some extent, as we've seen, counterculture
ideas and young people's hopes of overcoming "uptight" ways
of living have contributed to what is sometimes loosely described as "the new consciousness." Yet, as our look at the
emerging self-help patterns shows, those that are dominating
the current scene actually have little in common with the
alternative society youthful utopians hoped to achieve. Nor
indeed is it young people primarily who are flocking to the
growth programs and the psychological-help books. In fact,
much of the effort to keep self-awareness from overwhelming
social awareness may be attributed to the young. The communes and concern for the environment reflect the search
for new social forms more than a faith in form-free privatism.

At the same time, however, the huge popularity of meditation and related schemes among college students today suggests
the danger of their "graduating" into the more interiorizing versions of the self-help creed. We have heard a great deal
about how American middle-class youth are disenchanted,
uncommitted, alienated. The student movement so strong
during the 1960s supposedly no longer exists. Young people
today should be ripe for whatever personalistic or irrational
fads come onto the scene. And there may be some evidence
that this is so. Midge Decter, in her controversial book *Liberal Parents, Radical Children,* claims that today's middle-
class parents have bred a generation of egocentric and
unthinking self-styled revolutionaries and retreatists.⁵⁰ But if

youth today retreats inward, this may be due less to the permissiveness of liberals than to the aimlessness encouraged by
self-awareness gurus.

Railing against pot smoking and "easy sex" misses the
point. Young people have also adopted, as part of the liberal
legacy, humane values (of personal decency and social equality) and a healthy repudiation of cant and hypocrisy. We
have yet to see that they will not, in fact, make a better
society. Sociologist Richard Flacks has described youth revolt
as "a sign that a new culture and a new social order have been
placed on the agenda of history." But as he warns, this promise can only be fulfilled "if youth is transcended—if the young
and not-young who have a common interest in a new social
order come together to make their collective mark and help
each other realize their common dreams."[51]

If young people may be seen as embodying the promise of
a new society, old people are rarely viewed in such a light. In
fact overcoming the stereotyped notion that persons older
than 65 can no longer make productive contributions should
be one of their major goals. But older persons have other
collective interests as well. Retirement benefits, housing, and
medical care are among the most important. Concern over
failing health could make old people especially susceptible
to any schemes that promise to enhance their vitality and general well-being. So far there are relatively few signs of the
awareness commercializers cashing in on this particular market. Nor do the aged themselves seem to be showing great
interest in what they offer. On the contrary, this segment of
our population, more than ever before, is being politicized.
Through organizations like the National Association of Re-
tired Persons, the National Council of Senior Citizens, and
the Gray Panthers, old people are organizing, planning, and
engaging in sophisticated political lobbying.[52] Growing old
gracefully, they have recognized, presupposes the protection
of rights and advancement of interests through collective
action.

Preventive Awareness

The new healers invite all segments of the population to take advantage of their prescription for joy. They do not accept these distinctions of class or race. They oppose both the general tendency to classify and the subsuming of unique individuals under social roles. They reach out to all "humans." People in all social categories can benefit, and the sooner they're exposed to the new catechism the better. If kids can get in touch with their feelings at an early age, then many of the problems that now plague adults will never have to arise.

This call for preventive awareness naturally focuses on the schools. In a great many American communities, "affective education" is becoming the underground (sometimes, not-so-underground) curriculum. Encounter-groupers showed an early interest in schools, believing in particular that feelings-oriented rapping could improve student–staff communication and morale.[53] By plan, or informally through the proclivities of particular teachers, "human potential" and other self-fulfillment ideas and practices are now actively creeping into the classroom. These experiments in personal growth vary widely. Sometimes they occur more or less on a spur of the moment basis, when a teacher believes the time is ripe for a group exploration of feelings or some type of relaxation exercise. Sometimes they are built-in as an important component of the regular curriculum.

One recent book on awareness training in schools describes an elaborate program (DUSO—developing understanding of self and others), complete with manual, storybooks, posters, cassettes, puppets, and even its own theme-mascot ("Duso, the blue-and-white dolphin").[54] Another growth-for-school-kids book discusses a wide range of techniques for "emotional reeducation" (including "visualization" training, role-playing and psychodrama, "group fantasy," and meditation). A good example of how far this new learning may be carried is that author's suggestion of "empathizing with a nonhuman phenomenon" ("I want you to identify with the potassium in the bottle. How does it feel? What does it think?")![55] If such methods come to be widely accepted, we can expect the new fad of meditation to accompany them or to follow close behind. The Maharishi informs us that his technique will usher in a worldwide "educational renaissance," and the authors of a leading TM book claim higher motivation and increased achievement among meditating college students. They also report the preparation of "TM courses" for use in the primary schools.[56]

Often, when these self-exploration methods have been employed in the public schools, they have given rise to active community controversy. Critics have charged they are anti-intellectual, a waste of time, or else emotionally disturbing to the students. Users and advocates insist they make the learning experience more meaningful, that they help in eliciting student attention and the will to explore, and that they combat the syndrome of unhealthy authority relations that usually afflicts the schools and impedes education. And, of course, that they enhance creativity, optimize the achieving of potential, and increase vitality and enjoyment in the learning process.[57]

We have to recognize that in today's schools the new healers find a fertile field for experimentation. As a consequence of the now almost old-fashioned "progressive" movement, even nonradical educationists see the importance of what John Holt succinctly describes as "learner-directed, noncoercive, interest-inspired learning."[58] This broad acceptance of participation and learning-by-doing has been pushed still further through a variety of radical experiments and ideas. A. S. Neill's already-classic example of an anti-authoritarian school, Summerhill. A variety of model "free" schools and "open" schools, both at home and abroad. Counterculture-based criticism of educational institutions and programs. The radical call for "deschooling society" (abolishing compulsory education, and providing a wide range of learning alternatives), voiced most forcefully now by priest-prophet Ivan Illich, but developed earlier by such social critics as Paul Goodman.[59]

There is much to commend in these outlooks. Nowadays only very rigid conservatives would dispute the value of giving the student an opportunity to explore and build on his or her own interests and a sense of active participation in the educational process. Most teachers and school administrators recognize that "fact mongering," memorization, and the imposing of "lessons" are vastly inferior to other types of learning. Yet bringing the student into the educational process and making it more meaningful do not require a total abandonment of substance. As John Holt has emphasized, nonauthoritarian learning can be either unstructured or structured. Similarly, it can involve varying amounts of "content." Even the new self-sensitizing techniques, if used sparingly and with great care, might be a useful adjunct to the exploration of substantive questions and the development (if not transmission) of "knowledge." The danger is that the new methods could come close to displacing content altogether.

One example of this is the new educational fad of "values clarification."[60] Since the self-awareness focus typically directs us away from specific value issues, any technique that brings values to the fore could be seen as an advance. At first the idea behind values clarification seems to be to get students to think about various value-laden questions and controversies. They are given "exercises" (rank-ordering, sentence-completion, and the like) designed to bring out their feelings about many personal qualities and goals (such as aggressiveness, honesty, materialism). They are asked to record what they think of themselves, and how they would like to be. They may explore feelings about numerous "policy" issues (disarmament, free medical care, capital punishment, racial desegregation, etc.). And such devices may be supplemented by some drawn even more directly from the encounter-group tradition.

For example, group sessions in which the student is asked to try to grasp "the feelings behind the words" or to "empathize with the speaker."

It turns out, however, that this approach is not really interested in which values students prize, or in the substantive or rational bases for such choices. Instead, stress is placed on experiencing and understanding the very process of valuing. Clarifying and ordering values is seen as a content-free skill to be developed more or less in the abstract. Values clarification does seem to be directed a bit more toward the substance of social life than many of the self-awareness schemes. At least, it involves experiencing and exploring feelings *about something*, rather than just feelings. Getting schoolchildren to think about value questions, and to consider their personal priorities, is quite desirable. Yet how meaningful these exercises (which have been used also with adults) will be, must depend on the substantive context in which they're placed. For a child to say how he or she feels about capital punishment may be a good thing. But the value of such expressions varies tremendously, depending on how much he or she *knows* about the actual uses of capital punishment, and how much he or she has explored the social and moral implications of that practice.

Advocates of values clarification don't always make clear just how much of that sort of "content" should accompany the exercises they propose. In its absence, it seems absurd to speak of values being clarified. Fascination with the so-called value-clarification process can also blur one's vision with respect to what might be called evaluating values. Learning a neutral skill certainly in no way ensures that one will be a good person. Indeed, much evil has been done by persons who may have been very skillful at clarifying and ordering their values. Specific values and priorities can be bad. If values clarification is to have any real meaning (and not degenerate into a dangerously extreme relativism) this point, at least, must be stressed.

The matter of values suggests yet another possible danger in the spread of self-awareness outlooks to the schools. Much useful educational innovation—in some instances even involving application of these outlooks—has come about because of attempts in the inner-city schools to develop new ways of igniting the learning potential of poor and black children. Letting such students air their justified grievances. Activating their desire to learn. Finding a common ground to bridge the language and experiential gaps between them and more advantaged students and staff. To the extent such focus has been present, awareness-related efforts have amounted to considerably more than an encouragement of vague self-exploration. If that is to continue, the element of social consciousness must not be lost. This requires facing up to and dealing with class differences—something the new self-awareness specialists rarely do.

One of the more ominous possibilities is pointedly described by Jonathan Kozol, a most thoughtful advocate of radical educational change. Kozol stresses that reconstructing school programs cannot occur within a moral vacuum. If we aren't careful, innovation may become a plaything of the middle-class. "While children starve and others walk the city streets in fear on Monday afternoon, the privileged young people in the Free Schools of Vermont shuttle their hand-looms back and forth and speak of love and of 'organic processes.' They do 'their thing.' " Kozol's imagery may be harsh, but surely his point is well-taken: "an isolated upper-class Free School for the children of the white and rich within a land like the United States and in a time of torment . . . is a great deal too much like a sandbox for the children of the S.S. guards at Auschwitz."[61]

Formal education inevitably involves an intervention in the lives of children. It would be supremely ironic if innovators who say they hope to free children from earlier restrictive interventions simply imposed a new and equally limiting one. One of Thomas Szasz's strongest criticisms of psychiatric imperialism has concerned the movement for community mental health and the related expansion of preventive psychiatric care into the schools. Schoolkids are indeed a captive audience. When they are diagnosed, counseled, or tranquilized, or put into special "learning problem" groups, there isn't much they can do about it. Unlike the psychiatrists, the new healers aren't calling them "patients." But self-awareness thinking, as we've seen, carries a similar implication of personal deficiency. If being "together" is the new mental health, can the placement of children in "the program for marginally awares" be that far behind?

Above all, it would be a travesty of the educational process if the misguided outlooks discussed in this book were allowed to dominate what is taught in our schools. It is bad enough that adult Americans so gullibly accept these oversimplifications. To impose them on children would be tragic. Obviously, a little meditation, or body relaxation, or even sensitively guided rapping, will do little harm. Such practices, however, are less alarming than the notions that underlie them and that they reinforce. It won't hurt most kids to acknowledge their emotions a bit more, but we cannot allow them to grow up believing that this is all that counts in the world. A little awareness may be a dangerous thing. If this is not recognized in the schools, it may be difficult to repair the damage later on.

Conclusion

When I first thought about writing this book, I viewed the project with mixed feelings. I was already quite convinced that self-awareness ideas were misleading. That personal growth themes, if carried very far, could hamper efforts to accomplish meaningful social change. At the same time, an awful lot of people seemed to be getting some kind of satisfaction out of all this self-exploration. I was not eager to seem a killjoy. I did not wish to come across as sharing the views of conservative opponents of permissiveness. Finally, I was not at all certain that the developments on which I wanted to focus were of sufficient magnitude to warrant a full-scale dissection.

Thinking about all this again in retrospect, I believe I made the right decision. What has been happening, even during the past year or so, makes it eminently clear that the awareness trend is not about to go away. On the contrary, it is picking

up fantastic momentum. If encounter groups as such are not
as popular as they were in the 1950s and 1960s, new self-
realization schemes have been continuously popping up to
take their place. Virtually every day, another psychological-help
book built around the awareness outlook hits the book-
stores, and gets the "big treatment" in the mass media. Magazines more and more are featuring articles on self-exploration
theories and techniques. Today's advertising copy incorporates
a large measure of awareness jargon. Commercial exploiters
capitalize on the trend in new and ingenious ways. As I write
this, for example, jewelers announce the imminent marketing
of "the Mood Stone ring." Billed as a portable biofeedback
device, it is supposed to change color—depending on whether
you are relaxed, tense, excited, or what not. At $45 a shot, it
appears to be the latest thing in awareness chic.

If these were isolated and frivolous manifestations of personal whim, they would not be cause for alarm. But they are
not. People are taking these ideas and activities very seriously.
As I have tried to emphasize, the ideas are considerably more
dangerous than the activities themselves. And it is easy for
critics to overlook them. Encounter-grouping, for example,
has frequently been labeled anti-intellectual. Yet, it may be
even more useful to recognize that the awareness movement
propagates ideas of its own (including that of downgrading
intellect). Far from being nonexistent, awareness ideas are
now widely disseminated, especially through the mass-marketed guidance books. Unfortunately, many of these ideas are
simplistic and unsound.

Those of us who would like to see our society become more
egalitarian, less materialistic, and more seriously dedicated to
its professed social ideals, must greet with dismay the expansion of these outlooks. America suffers already from an over-
eager acceptance of the doctrines of individualism. The new
irrationalism could deal a death blow to any prospects that
still exist for reconstructing our rightly criticized and not
much enjoyed way of life. Asserting a warmed-over version

of the American dream (with a few "therapeutic" and a few "Eastern" touches added) will only ensure more of the same. Belief in self-help as the major path to social change is an illusion. The so-called visionaries and therapists who teach this belief engage in something much more akin to fantasy than to true vision. Self-preoccupation *instead of* social change is the likely outcome.

As I have stressed, the new helpers largely ignore the real problems of American society. Some of us may be able to afford $45 "mood stones" and $125 meditation courses. Yet the United States is almost unique among industrialized nations in not having a comprehensive free health care program. Many Americans apparently enjoy reading of the "crises" of "relating" or of being "creative." While they are doing so, hundreds of thousands of their fellow citizens are out of work and scraping to make ends meet. White middle-class awareness enthusiasts amuse themselves with yoga and body relaxation, at the indirect expense of blacks, Chicanos, and American Indians—whose real suffering is ignored. As we've seen, even women (whose suffering may be more subtle) are ultimately short-changed by the movement.

Indeed we are all short-changed to the extent we adopt its limiting perspectives. What the new helpers don't seem to realize is that we can't be aware of ourselves unless we're aware of our surroundings. There can be no real self-awareness without social awareness. Yet this is precisely what is missing in the new credo. Social consciousness has never been a strong point of Americans. The outlooks examined in this book both reflect and reinforce our culture's long-standing resistance to social and political frames of reference. Awareness facilitators believe they are in some vanguard when they refuse to think in terms of class distinctions and social institutions. In fact, they are simply evading reality. These elements of our social order may indeed (in their present forms) be "arbitrary." That does not make their effects any the less real. Facing up to their existence leads to a recognition of shared interests and of the need for collective action to produce change. Whenever we begin to consider how to ameliorate specific problems of people in our society, the superficiality and emptiness of awareness thinking quickly become apparent.

We are also in peril of being "facilitated" out of whatever glimmerings of social conscience now inform our behavior. Americans are pragmatists, but they're also supposed to be idealists of a sort. A disdain for forms and "content" does more than blind us to how present-day society really works. It distracts us from basic questions of morality and justice. From asking what society ought to be like, and how individuals ought to behave. Concern for issues of this kind gives way to cynicism and interpersonal manipulation. There is much talk about taking "responsibility" for oneself, but little attention to the placing of responsibility for the shape of the society in which we live and which we all sustain. That people might gain a large measure of self-fulfillment precisely by taking their social responsibilities seriously, never seems to occur to the current self-fulfillment experts.

The new quest inwards, if kept in proper perspective, might in some ways prove quite beneficial. Yoga may do things for people that jogging can't do. Daily meditation seems clearly preferable to a daily dose of tranquilizers. Many of us could use a little "freeing up" emotionally, and increased exercise of our creative faculties. The real danger is that the quest will not be kept in reasonable perspective. That our search for an easy solution to all our troubles will overwhelm our caution and our commonsense. That confused and short-sighted notions about life and society will begin to influence all our attitudes and behavior. Popularizers of the awareness view often encourage this with their glib pronouncements and wildly excessive claims. They must not be allowed to go unchallenged.

Notes

Introduction: The Awareness Craze

1. Alvin Toffler, *Future Shock* (New York: Bantam Books, 1971), p. 226.
2. The statements appeared in advertisements published in *The Village Voice* on (respectively) June 30, 1975, p. 37, and June 23, 1975, p. 44.
3. Advertisement for The New School, in *The New York Times*, January 6, 1975, p. 18.

I. Feeling Your Feelings

1. Claudio Naranjo, *The One Quest* (New York: Ballantine Books, 1972), p. 23. I am grateful to Owen Schur for bringing this book to my attention.
2. *Ibid.*, p. 4.
3. Theodore Roszak, *Where the Wasteland Ends* (Garden City, N.Y.: Doubleday Anchor Books, 1973), p. xxii.
4. See Robert Hunter, *The Storming of the Mind* (Garden City, N.Y.: Doubleday Anchor Books, 1972), especially Ch. 14.
5. Alan Watts, *The Book* (New York: Vintage Books, 1972), p. 9.
6. Kurt W. Back, *Beyond Words* (Baltimore, Md.: Penguin Books, 1973), p. 221. For a recent view of encounter groups as totalitarian brainwashing, see Andrew Malcolm, *Tyranny of the Group* (Totowa, N.J.: Littlefield, Adams and Co., 1975).
7. See Thomas J. Cottle, "Exposing Ourselves in Public," *The New Republic* (March 8, 1975).

8. Jane Howard, *Please Touch* (New York: Delta Books, 1970), p. 248.
9. William C. Schutz, *Joy* (New York: Grove Press, Evergreen Black Cat Books, 1969), p. 24. See also Jane Howard, above, for personal impressions of many of the techniques.
10. Frederick Perls, Ralph F. Hefferline, and Paul Goodman, *Gestalt Therapy* (New York: Delta Books, 1951), p. 105.
11. Jerry Greenwald, *Be the Person You Were Meant to Be* (New York: Simon and Schuster, 1973), p. 13.
12. Richard E. Johnson, "The Future of Humanistic Psychology," *The Humanist* (March/April 1975), p. 7.
13. Robert E. Ornstein, in Claudio Naranjo and Robert E. Ornstein, *On the Psychology of Meditation* (New York: Viking Press, 1971), p. 194.
14. Alan Watts, *Psychotherapy East and West* (New York: Ballantine Books, 1961), p. 57.
15. Maharishi Mahesh Yogi, *Transcendental Meditation* [formerly, *The Science of Being and Art of Living*] (New York: Signet Books, 1968), p. 43.
16. Watts, *Psychotherapy East and West*, op. cit., p. 39.
17. Schutz, *Joy*, op. cit., p. 28; and see all of his Ch. 2.
18. Alexander Lowen, *Pleasure* (New York and Baltimore, Md.: Penguin Books, 1975), p. 120.
19. Robert E. Ornstein, *The Psychology of Consciousness* (San Francisco: W. H. Freeman and Co., 1972), pp. 154–155.
20. Marvin Karlins and Lewis M. Andrews, *Biofeedback* (New York: Warner Paperback Library, 1973), p. 19.
21. Harold H. Bloomfield, Michael Peter Cain, and Dennis T. Jaffee, *TM* (New York: Delacorte Press, 1975), p. 7.
22. *Ibid.*, pp. 3, 56.
23. Frederick S. Perls, *Gestalt Therapy Verbatim* (New York: Bantam Books, 1971), p. 23.
24. Joel Latner, *The Gestalt Therapy Book* (New York: Bantam Books, 1974), pp. 16, 17.
25. Perls, *Gestalt Therapy Verbatim*, op. cit., p. 6.
26. Arthur Janov, *The Primal Scream* (New York: Dell Publishing Co., 1972), p. 17.
27. Greenwald, *Be the Person You Were Meant to Be*, op. cit., especially, pp. 23–36.
28. This discussion is based on Lowen, *Pleasure*, cited above.
29. Paul A. Robinson, *The Freudian Left* (New York: Harper Colophon Books, 1970), p. 23.

II. *Achieving Sensory Success*

1. Latner, *The Gestalt Therapy Book*, op. cit., pp. 173–174.
2. Nena and George O'Neill, *Shifting Gears* (New York: Avon Books, 1975), p. 101.
3. Barrie and Charlotte Hopson, *Intimate Feedback* (New York: Simon and Schuster, 1975), p. 34.
4. Lowen, *Pleasure*, op. cit., pp. 68–69.
5. Janov, *The Primal Scream*, op. cit., pp. 21, 34, 37, 49.
6. Russell Jacoby, *Social Amnesia* (Boston: Beacon Press, 1975), p. 17.
7. Frederick S. Perls, "Four Lectures," in *Gestalt Therapy Now*, Joel Fagan and Irma Lee Shepard eds., (New York: Harper Colophon Books, 1971), p. 14.
8. Philip Slater, *Earthwalk* (Garden City, N.Y.: Doubleday Anchor Books, 1974), p. 115.
9. Watts, *The Book*, op. cit., p. 72.
10. Maharishi Mahesh Yogi, *Transcendental Meditation*, op. cit., p. 84.
11. Ornstein, *The Psychology of Consciousness*, op. cit., Chs. 6 and 7.
12. Nena and George O'Neill, *Open Marriage* (New York: Avon Books, 1973), pp. 75–80.
13. Greenwald, *Be the Person You Were Meant to Be*, op. cit., pp. 64, 157–158.
14. Charles A. Reich, *The Greening of America* (New York: Bantam Books, 1971), Ch. XI.
15. Janov, *The Primal Scream*, op. cit., pp. 105, 221, 245.
16. Mildred Newman and Bernard Berkowitz, with Jean Owen, *How to Be Your Own Best Friend* (New York: Ballantine Books, 1974), pp. 54–55.
17. Perls, *Gestalt Therapy Verbatim*, op. cit., p. 3.
18. Hopson, *Intimate Feedback*, op. cit., p. 73.
19. Carlos Castaneda, *The Teachings of Don Juan* (New York: Ballantine Books, 1969), especially pp. 246–255.
20. Ornstein, *The Psychology of Consciousness*, op. cit., Ch. 3 and pp. 136–140.
21. Watts, *The Book*, op. cit., p. 109.
22. David Solomon, ed., *LSD: The Consciousness Expanding Drug* (New York: G. P. Putnam-Berkley Medallion Books, 1966), p. viii.
23. Hunter, *The Storming of the Mind*, op. cit., p. 99.
24. Tom Wolfe, *The Electric Kool Aid Acid Test* (New York: Bantam Books, 1969), p. 40.

25. Ornstein, *The Psychology of Consciousness,* op. cit., p. 158.
26. R. D. Laing, *The Politics of Experience* (New York: Ballantine Books, 1968), pp. 133, 190.
27. Abraham H. Maslow, *Toward a Psychology of Being,* 2nd ed. (New York: D. Van Nostrand Co., 1968), p. 11.
28. Maharishi Mahesh Yogi, *Transcendental Meditation,* op. cit., p. 81.
29. Jacoby, *Social Amnesia,* op. cit., p. 49.
30. Maslow, *Toward a Psychology of Being,* op. cit., Ch. 6, "Cognition of Being in the Peak-Experience."
31. The above discussion is based on *ibid.,* Ch. 10, "Creativity in Self-Actualizing People."
32. A recent book explicitly combining the pottery and awareness usages is M. C. Richards, *Centering* (Middletown, Conn.: Wesleyan University Press, 1964).
33. Perls, *Gestalt Therapy Verbatim,* op. cit., p. 40.
34. A good collection of various literary, and other personal statements on drug use is David Ebin, ed., *The Drug Experience* (New York: Grove Press, Evergreen Books, 1961).
35. Arthur Sainer, *The Radical Theatre Notebook* (New York: Avon Books, 1975), pp. 17–52.
36. Robert J. Pierce, "The Anna Halprin Story: Dancing in the Streets, in Prisons, in Hallways," *The Village Voice* (March 10, 1975), pp. 93–95.
37. Janie Rhyne, "The Gestalt Art Experience," in *Gestalt Therapy Now,* Fagan and Shepard, eds., op. cit., p. 274.
38. Reich, *The Greening of America,* op. cit., p. 260.
39. Hunter, *The Storming of the Mind,* op. cit., p. 72.

III. *Learning To Be Real*

1. The three quotes are taken, respectively, from Perls, "Four Lectures," in *Gestalt Therapy Now,* Fagan and Shepard, eds., op. cit., p. 17; Watts, *Psychotherapy East and West,* op. cit., p. 21; and O'Neill, *Shifting Gears,* op. cit., p. 245.
2. Reich, *The Greening of America,* op. cit., p. 83.
3. On these "internal" approaches see Alexander Lowen, *The Betrayal of the Body* (New York: Collier Books, 1969), Ch. 13, "The Achievement of Identity"; Janov, *The Primal Scream,* op. cit., especially pp. 31–32; and Thomas A. Harris, *I'm OK—You're OK* (New York: Avon Books, 1973), Chs. 2–5. Also Eric Berne, *Games People Play* (New York: Grove Press, 1964).

4. On the "self" see especially George H. Mead, *Mind, Self and Society.* (Chicago: University of Chicago Press, 1934); also Chad Gordon and Kenneth J. Gergen, eds., *The Self in Social Interaction* (New York: Wiley, 1968).

5. Newman and Berkowitz, *How to Be Your Own Best Friend,* op. cit., pp. 22–26.

6. Greenwald, *Be the Person You Were Meant to Be,* op. cit., p. 17.

7. Norman Vincent Peale, *The Power of Positive Thinking* (Greenwich, Conn.: Fawcett Crest Books, 1956).

8. Bloomfield, Cain, and Jaffee, *TM,* op. cit., p. 10.

9. Will Herberg, *Protestant-Catholic-Jew* (Garden City, N.Y.: Doubleday Anchor Books, 1960), p. 260.

10. Greenwald, *Be the Person You Were Meant to Be,* op. cit., pp. 16, 101.

11. Albert Ellis, *Humanistic Psychotherapy* (New York: McGraw-Hill, 1973), pp. 39–40.

12. William Glasser, *Reality Therapy* (New York: Harper Colophon Books, 1975), p. 30.

13. O'Neill, *Shifting Gears,* op. cit., p. 236.

14. Newman and Berkowitz, *How to Be Your Own Best Friend,* op. cit., p. 89.

15. *Ibid.,* p. 28.

16. "Book Ends," *The New York Times Book Review* (May 18, 1975), p. 53.

17. Jacket streamer for Herbert Fensterheim and Jean Baer, *Don't Say Yes When You Want to Say No* (New York: McKay, 1975).

18. Advertisement for Manuel J. Smith, *When I Say No, I Feel Guilty.* (New York: Dial Press, 1975), appearing in *The New York Times Book Review,* February 9, 1975.

19. Fensterheim and Baer, *Don't Say Yes When You Want to Say No,* op. cit., Ch. 1.

20. *Ibid.,* Ch. 3.

21. *Ibid.,* p. 35.

22. As quoted by Howard Smith and Brian Van Der Horst, "Scenes," *The Village Voice* (February 3, 1975), p. 18. See also Marsha Dubrow, "Female Assertiveness: How a Pussycat Can Learn to Be a Panther," *New York Magazine* (July 28, 1975).

23. Lowen, *Pleasure,* op. cit., pp. 152–160.

24. The discussion that follows is based on O'Neill, *Shifting Gears,* op. cit., pp. 20–21, 26–28, 104–106, and *passim.*

25. For a review of theories and findings relating to social class, see T. B. Bottomore, *Classes in Modern Society* (New York: Pan-

theon, 1966); also, Kurt B. Mayer and Walter Buckley, *Class and Society*, 3rd. ed. (New York: Random House, 1970).
26. Roszak, *Where the Wasteland Ends*, op. cit., pp. 380, 381, 386.
27. Karl Marx, *The German Ideology* (1845–6), as quoted in T. B. Bottomore and M. Rubel, eds., *Karl Marx: Selected Writings in Sociology and Social Philosophy* (London: Watts and Co., 1956), p. 75.
28. Reich, *The Greening of America*, op. cit., pp. 327, 329, 330, 334.

IV. *The Mystique of Relating*

1. As quoted in Theodore Roszak, *The Making of a Counter Culture* (Garden City, N.Y.: Doubleday Anchor Books, 1969), pp. 58–59.
2. The quotes are, respectively, from Philip Slater, *The Pursuit of Loneliness* (Boston: Beacon Press, 1970), p. 8; and Slater, *Earthwalk*, op. cit., p. 83.
3. Schutz, *Joy*, op. cit., pp. 198–210.
4. Janov, *The Primal Scream*, op. cit., p. 167.
5. Naranjo and Ornstein, *On the Psychology of Meditation*, op. cit., pp. 170–212.
6. Maslow, *Toward a Psychology of Being*, op. cit., pp. 42, 43, 74–78.
7. O'Neill, *Shifting Gears*, op. cit., p. 214.
8. O'Neill, *Open Marriage*, op. cit., p. 40.
9. George Gilder, *Sexual Suicide* (New York: Bantam Books, 1975), pp. 51, 62.
10. *Ibid.*, pp. 259, 260.
11. For a good overall review of these and other types of evidence see Vivian Gornick and Barbara K. Moran, eds., *Woman in Sexist Society* (New York: Signet Books, 1972).
12. Gilder, *Sexual Suicide*, op. cit., p. 47.
13. In Perls, *Gestalt Therapy Verbatim*, frontispiece.
14. O'Neill, *Open Marriage*, op. cit., pp. 253–256.
15. Robert N. Whitehurst, "Alternative Life-Styles," *The Humanist* (May-June, 1975), p. 25.
16. George Gilder, *Naked Nomads* (New York: Quadrangle/The New York Times Book Co., 1974), p. 74.
17. Berne, *Games People Play*, op. cit., pp. 13–34. See also his more technical *Transactional Analysis in Psychotherapy* (New York: Grove Press, 1961).
18. *Ibid.*, pp. 48, 61, 105, 171–172, 184.
19. Erving Goffman, *The Presentation of Self in Everyday Life* (Garden City, N.Y.: Doubleday Anchor Books, 1959).

20. Harris, *I'm OK—You're OK*, op. cit., pp. 54, 74, 152.
21. George R. Bach and Peter Wyden, *The Intimate Enemy* (New York: Avon Books, 1970), pp. 19, 31, 64, 83, 328.
22. George R. Bach and Ronald M. Deutsch, *Pairing* (New York: Avon Books, 1971), pp. 13, 14, 103–115, 159, 241, 271–272.
23. Julius Fast, *Body Language* (New York: Pocket Books, 1971), pp. 83–92, 175–176, 180.
24. Hopson, *Intimate Feedback*, op. cit., p. 19.
25. *Ibid., passim.*
26. Maslow, *Toward a Psychology of Being*, op. cit., p. 79.
27. Greenwald, *Be the Person You Were Meant to Be*, op. cit., p. 207.
28. Slater, *Earthwalk*, op. cit., p. 123.

V. *Women and Awareness*

1. Stephanie Harrington, "Ms. Versus Cosmo: Two Faces of the Same Eve," *The New York Times Magazine* (August 11, 1974), pp. 10, 76.
2. Phyllis Chesler, *Women and Madness* (New York: Avon Books, 1972), p. 109.
3. Judith Hole and Ellen Levine, *Rebirth of Feminism* (New York: Quadrangle/The New York Times Book Co., 1971), p. 207.
4. Sheila Rowbotham, *Women's Consciousness, Man's World* (Harmondsworth, Middlesex, England: Penguin Books, 1973), pp. 85–89, 90. See also Ann Oakley, *The Sociology of Housework* (New York: Pantheon, 1975).
5. Ingrid Bengis, *Combat in the Erogenous Zone* (New York: Bantam Books, 1973), p. 59.
6. *Ibid.*, pp. 4–5.
7. Hole and Levine, *Rebirth of Feminism*, op. cit., p. 237.
8. Naomi Weisstein, "Psychology Constructs the Female," in *Woman in Sexist Society*, op. cit., Gornick and Moran, eds., p. 209.
9. See for example the more favorable interpretation of Freudianism in Juliet Mitchell, *Psychoanalysis and Feminism* (New York: Vintage Books, 1975).
10. Gornick and Moran, "Introduction," to *Woman in Sexist Society*, op. cit., p. xviii.
11. Lowen, *Pleasure*, op. cit., pp. 225–226.
12. See for example discussion by Alex Shulman, "Organs and Orgasms," in Gornick and Moran, *Woman in Sexist Society*.

13. See Linda Wolfe, "Funny Valentine," *New York Magazine* (February 17, 1975), pp. 70–71; also Lonnie Garfield Barbach, *For Yourself* (Garden City, N.Y.: Doubleday, 1975).

14. See Linda Wolfe, *Playing Around* (New York: William Morrow, 1975).

15. Chesler, *Women and Madness*, op. cit., p. 90.

16. See Ellen Frankfort, *Vaginal Politics* (New York: Quadrangle/ The New York Times Book Co., 1972).

17. Rowbotham, *Women's Consciousness, Man's World*, op. cit., pp. 41–42.

18. Weisstein, "Psychology Constructs the Female," op. cit., p. 222.

19. Gilder, *Naked Nomads*, op. cit., p. 149.

20. Rowbotham, *Women's Consciousness, Man's World*, op. cit., pp. 34–35.

21. Shulamith Firestone, *The Dialectic of Sex* (New York: Bantam Books, 1971), p. 36.

22. Kate Millett, *Sexual Politics* (New York: Avon Books, 1971), p. 63.

23. Juliet Mitchell, *Woman's Estate* (New York: Vintage Books, 1973), pp. 21, 35.

24. "Politics of the Ego: A Manifesto for New York Radical Feminists" (1969), in *Woman in Sexist Society*, Gornick and Moran, eds., op. cit., pp. 440–441.

25. Mitchell, *Woman's Estate*, op. cit., p. 38.

26. See Claudia Dreifus, *Woman's Fate: Raps From a Feminist Consciousness-Raising Group* (New York: Bantam Books, 1973), pp. 30–35.

27. Kathie Sarachild, "A Program for Feminist 'Consciousness Raising,'" *Notes 2* (1968), as quoted in Hole and Levine, *Rebirth of Feminism*, op. cit., p. 131.

28. Dreifus, *Woman's Fate*, op. cit., p. 6.

29. *Ibid.*, p. 7.

30. Gornick and Moran, "Introduction," op. cit., p. xxi.

31. Mitchell, *Woman's Estate*, op. cit., p. 63.

32. Dreifus, *Woman's Fate*, p. 18.

33. Representative findings can be found in Gornick and Moran, op. cit., Hole and Levine, op. cit., and Robin Morgan, ed., *Sisterhood is Powerful* (New York: Vintage Books, 1970). See also *Women's Role in Contemporary Society*, the Report of the New York City Commission on Human Rights, September 1970 (New York: Avon Books, 1972). On legal aspects see Karen DeCrow, *Sexist Justice* (New York: Vintage Books, 1974).

34. Eleanor Holmes Norton, "Introduction," to *Women's Role in Contemporary Society*, pp. 26, 27.
35. *Ibid.*, pp. 29–45.
36. Hole and Levine, *Rebirth of Feminism*, op. cit., Part III, "Areas of Action."
37. Mitchell, *Woman's Estate*, op. cit., Part Two, "The Oppression of Women."
38. Gornick and Moran, op. cit., "Introduction," p. xx.
39. Una Stannard, "The Mask of Beauty," in Gornick and Moran, op. cit., p. 194.
40. *Ibid.*, p. 195.

VI. Therapy More or Less

1. See especially Thomas S. Szasz, *The Myth of Mental Illness* (New York: Harper & Row, 1961); *Law, Liberty, and Psychiatry* (New York: Macmillan, 1963); and *The Manufacture of Madness* (New York: Harper & Row, 1970). Also, Edwin M. Schur, "Psychiatrists Under Attack," *The Atlantic Monthly* (June 1966), pp. 72–76; and E. Fuller Torrey, *The Death of Psychiatry* (New York: Penguin Books, 1975).
2. Maslow, *Toward a Psychology of Being*, op. cit., Preface, and Addendum: "The Eupsychian Network."
3. This point is emphasized by the (closely related) "existential" psychiatrists. See Rollo May, ed., *Existence* (New York: Simon and Schuster, 1952).
4. Kurt Back, *Beyond Words*, op. cit., p. 221; see also Andrew Malcolm, *The Tyranny of the Group*, op. cit., Ch. 7, "The Casualty Rate."
5. Malcolm, p. 104.
6. *Ibid.*, p. 74.
7. Jacoby, *Social Amnesia*, op. cit., p. 139.
8. Gordon P. Holleb and Walter H. Abrams, *Alternatives in Community Mental Health* (Boston: Beacon Press, 1975), p. 29. I am grateful to Estelle Disch, of Pequod, for bringing this book to my attention.
9. *Ibid.*, pp. 4–5.
10. *Ibid.*, pp. 76, 119, 120, 136.
11. Bloomfield, Cain, and Jaffee, *TM*, op. cit., p. 192.
12. See Back, *Beyond Words*, op. cit., especially Ch. 4, "Chronicles of the Movement." Also, Schutz, *Joy*, op. cit., Ch. 5, "Organizational Relations." A representative sample of research papers in

this area is Harvey A. Hornstein, et al., eds., *Social Intervention* (New York: Free Press, 1971).

13. Karlins and Andrews, *Biofeedback*, op. cit., p. 18.
14. Back, *Beyond Words*, op. cit., pp. 192–193.
15. Georgia Dullea, "Married Couples Take New Look at Life Together," *The New York Times* (June 24, 1975), p. 38.
16. Howard, *Please Touch*, op. cit., p. 107.
17. Back, *Beyond Words*, op. cit., p. 183.
18. *Carl Rogers on Encounter Groups* (New York: Harper & Row, Harrow Books, 1973), p. 152.
19. Maharishi Mahesh Yogi, *Transcendental Meditation*, op. cit., p. 236.
20. Janov, *The Primal Scream*, op. cit., p. 169.
21. Bloomfield, Cain, and Jaffee, *TM*, op. cit., pp. 106–107.
22. Lewis Yablonsky, *Synanon: The Tunnel Back* (New York: Macmillan, 1964).
23. Howard, *Please Touch*, op. cit., p. 73.
24. Yablonsky, *Synanon: The Tunnel Back*, op. cit., p. vi.
25. Daniel Casriel and Grover Amen, *Daytop* (New York: Hill and Wang, 1971), p. x.
26. Yablonsky, *Synanon: The Tunnel Back*, op. cit., p. 368.
27. See Isidor Chein, et al., *The Road to H* (New York: Basic Books, 1964). Also Edwin M. Schur, *Our Criminal Society* (Englewood Cliffs, N.J.: Prentice-Hall, 1969).
28. Herbert Packer, "The Crime Tariff," in Packer, *The Limits of the Criminal Sanction* (Stanford: Stanford University Press, 1968). See also Alfred R. Lindesmith, *The Addict and the Law* (Bloomington: Indiana University Press, 1965).
29. For data and arguments bearing on these points see Edwin M. Schur and Hugo Adam Bedau, *Victimless Crimes: Two Sides of a Controversy* (Englewood Cliffs, N.J.: Prentice-Hall, 1974).
30. *Ibid.*, pp. 26–28. See also Edward M. Brecher, et al., *Licit and Illicit Drugs* (Boston: Little, Brown, 1972); and *Dealing With Drug Abuse: A Report to the Ford Foundation* (New York: Praeger, 1972).
31. "Methadone and Jobs," *The New York Times* (August 20, 1975), p. 32. The statement in the court's ruling is by Judge Thomas P. Griesa.
32. Harris, *I'm OK—You're OK*, op. cit., pp. 72–73.
33. Schur, *Our Criminal Society*, op. cit., especially pp. 61–73 ("Are Criminals Sick?").
34. Maharishi Mahesh Yogi, *Transcendental Meditation*, op. cit., p. 310.

35. Bloomfield, Cain, and Jaffee, *TM*, op. cit., pp. 193–202.
36. As reported by Wayne King, in *The New York Times* (January 26, 1975), p. 39.
37. See Edwin M. Schur, *Radical Nonintervention: Rethinking the Delinquency Problem* (Englewood Cliffs, N.J.: Prentice-Hall, 1973), pp. 54–70.
38. Yablonsky, *Synanon: The Tunnel Back*, op. cit., Ch. 15, "Breakthrough in Correction."
39. *The Challenge of Crime in a Free Society*, President's Commission on Law Enforcement and Administration of Justice (Washington: U.S. Government Printing Office, 1967), p. 1.
40. Michael Harrington, *The Other America* (Baltimore, Md.: Penguin Books, 1963), p. 25.
41. Schur, *Our Criminal Society*, op. cit., pp. 9–12.
42. Richard Quinney, *Critique of Legal Order* (Boston: Little, Brown, 1973); also see Schur and Bedau, *Victimless Crime*, op. cit.
43. Gilder, *Sexual Suicide*, op. cit., p. 238.
44. Herbert Hendin, "Homosexuality and the Family," *The New York Times* (August 22, 1975), p. 31.
45. Dennis Altman, *Homosexual: Oppression and Liberation* (New York: Avon Books, 1971), p. 182.
46. On the gay liberation movement generally see Laud Humphreys, *Out of the Closets* (Englewood Cliffs, N.J.: Prentice-Hall, 1972); and Altman, *Homosexual: Oppression and Liberation.*
47. Harrington, *The Other America*, op. cit., p. 23.
48. *The New York Times Magazine* (February 9, 1975).
49. For a good discussion of these issues see Richard A. Cloward and Frances Fox Piven, *The Politics of Turmoil* (New York: Vintage Books, 1975).
50. Midge Decter, *Liberal Parents, Radical Children* (New York: Coward, McCann and Geoghegan, 1975).
51. Richard Flacks, *Youth and Social Change* (Chicago: Markham Pub. Co., 1971), p. 139.
52. See Nancy Hicks, "The Organized Elderly: A New Political Power," *The New York Times* (June 22, 1975), p. 1.
53. See for example Schutz, *Joy*, op. cit., pp. 215–236; and *Carl Rogers on Encounter Groups*, op. cit., pp. 154–161.
54. Clark E. Moustakas and Cereta Perry, *Learning to Be Free* (Englewood Cliffs, N.J.: Prentice-Hall, 1973), especially pp. 62–68.
55. John Mann, *Learning to Be* (New York: The Free Press, 1972), pp. 44–45. See also George B. Leonard, *Education and Ecstasy* (New York: Dell Books, 1968).

56. Maharishi Mahesh Yogi, *Transcendental Meditation,* op. cit., p. 309; Bloomfield, Cain, and Jaffee, *TM,* op. cit., pp. 202–213.
57. On such controversies see Howard, *Please Touch,* op. cit., pp. 156–165; and Malcolm, *The Tyranny of the Group,* op. cit., pp. 150–155.
58. John Holt, *Freedom and Beyond* (New York: Dell Pub. Co., 1972), p. 10.
59. For discussion of such developments see *Summerhill: For and Against* (New York: Hart Pub. Co., 1970); Holt, *Freedom and Beyond;* Jonathan Kozol, *Free Schools* (New York: Bantam Books, 1972); Ivan Illich, *Deschooling Society* (New York: Harper & Row, Harrow Books, 1972); Paul Goodman, *Growing Up Absurd* (New York: Vintage Books, 1962).
60. Sidney B. Simon, Leland W. Howe, and Howard Kirschenbaum, *Values Clarification* (New York: Hart Pub. Co., 1972).
61. Kozol, *Free Schools,* op. cit., p. 11.

Index